HOLT SCIENCE

D0930826

Abruscato • Fusco • Hassard • Peck • Strange

Holt, Rinehart and Winston, Inc.

Austin • New York • San Diego • Chicago • Toronto • Montreal

The Authors

Joseph Abruscato
Associate Dean
College of Education and Social Services
University of Vermont
Burlington, Vermont

Joan Fusco
Teacher
Pointview Elementary School
Westerville City Schools
Westerville, Ohio

Jack Hassard
Professor
College of Education
Georgia State University
Atlanta, Georgia

Donald Peck
Director
Center for Elementary Science
Fairleigh Dickinson University
Madison, New Jersey

Johanna Strange
Assistant Professor
Model Laboratory School
Eastern Kentucky University
Richmond, Kentucky

Photo and Art Credits start on page 292

Cover Photos: Bobcat—Tom McHugh, Photo Researchers

Saguaro cactus and cliffs in Arizona—Emil Muench, Photo Researchers

The bobcat is a wild cat that lives in the forests, mountains, swamps, and deserts of North America. Like many other cats, it hunts for food at night.

Requests for permission to make copies of any part of the work should be mailed to: Permissions, Holt, Rinehart and Winston, Inc., 1627 Woodland Avenue, Austin, Texas 78741
Printed in the United States of America
ISBN 0-03-011389-X

90 071 9876543

Acknowledgments

Teacher Consultants

Sister de Montfort Babb, I.H.M.
Science Teacher
Bishop O'Hara High School
Dunmore, Pennsylvania

Ernest Bibby
Science Consultant
Granville County Board of Education
Oxford, North Carolina

Linda C. Cardwell
Science Coordinator
Grand Prairie I.S.D.
Grand Prairie, Texas

James A. Harris
Principal
Rothschild Elementary School
Rothschild, Wisconsin

Rachel P. Keziah
Instructional Supervisor
New Hanover County Schools
Wilmington, North Carolina

Raymond E. Sanders, Jr.
Science Supervisor
Calcasieu Parish Schools
Lake Charles, Louisiana

Safety Consultant

Franklin D. Kizer
Executive Secretary
Council of State Science Supervisors, Inc.
Lancaster, Virginia

Special Education Consultant

Joan Baltman
Assistant Principal, Special Education
P.S. 177Q Elementary School
Queens, New York

Health Consultants

Mary C. Davis
Teacher
Tallapoosa County Schools
Dadeville, Alabama

A. Mark Riley
Science Department Chairperson
Eli Whitney Middle School
Tulsa Public Schools
Tulsa, Oklahoma

Diane E. Rushing
Teacher of Gifted and Talented
East Baton Rouge Parish Schools
Baton Rouge, Louisiana

Merita Lee Thompson, Ed.D.
Professor of Health Education
Eastern Kentucky University
Richmond, Kentucky

Content Consultants

John B. Jenkins
Professor of Biology
Swarthmore College
Swarthmore, Pennsylvania

Mark M. Payne, O.S.B.
Physics Teacher
St. Benedict's Preparatory School
Newark, New Jersey

Robert W. Ridky, Ph.D.
Professor of Geology
University of Maryland
College Park, Maryland

Contents

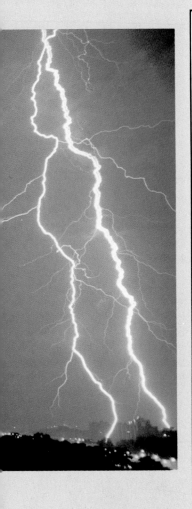

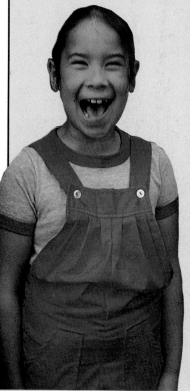

Unit 1

This picture shows a bird and a rhinoceros.

These animals do not eat the same things.

How else are they different?

LOOKING AHEAD

Look at the pictures in this unit.

Which animals would make good pets?

Tell why you think so.

Look at the frog and the insect.

How does each one move?

How else are they different?

Chapter 1

Animal Groups

1.

MAMMALS

All of these animals are **mammals.**
How are they the same? All mammals
have **hair** or **fur.** The hair helps them
keep warm. Mammals are **warm-blooded**
animals. The weather may be cold or
warm. But their bodies always stay the
same. Even when it is cold outside, their
bodies are warm.

All mammals are born alive. The babies drink milk from their mother. Mother mammals take care of their babies. All mammals breathe air with their **lungs**.

Mammals are different in some ways. They eat different foods. The mother dog eats meat. Some mammals eat only meat. Lions eat only meat.

Rabbits eat only plants.

Raccoons eat both plants and small animals.

What to do

A. Find some pictures of mammals.

B. Put the pictures into three groups.

- Mammals That Eat Plants
- Mammals That Eat Animals
- Mammals That Eat Plants and Animals

What do you see?

1. Which mammals eat plants?

2. Which mammals eat animals?

3. Which mammals eat plants and animals?

What do you think?

4. Do all mammals eat the same things?

2.

BIRDS

An eagle is **a bird.** Birds are animals
with **feathers** and **wings.** The eagle's
feathers help keep it warm and dry. The
large wings help it to fly. What other
birds do you know?

Birds are the same in many ways. All birds lay eggs. The mother bird lays her eggs in a nest. The mother or father sits on the eggs. This keeps them warm.

Soon babies hatch from the eggs.
The parents take care of their babies.
Do you know how?

All birds are warm-blooded. Even in winter, their bodies are warm. Birds breathe air with their lungs. How are birds and mammals the same? How are they different?

Look at all the birds again. They all have **beaks.** Are all the beaks the same shape? How does each bird use its beak?

What to do

A. Collect some feathers.

B. Look at the feathers. Feel them.

C. Put a drop of water on each one.

What do you see?

1. Tell what happened to the water on each feather.

What do you think?

2. Do you think birds get wet when it rains? Why?

3. What is another way that feathers are important to a bird?

3.

FISH

Many different kinds of animals live in water. **Fish** are animals that live in water. They use their tails and **fins** to swim. Some fish live in rivers and lakes.

Many fish live in the ocean. The seahorse is an ocean fish. It swims upright in shallow water. Do you see the fins and tail on this fish?

Fish are special water animals. They are covered by hard **scales.** The scales help protect the fish.

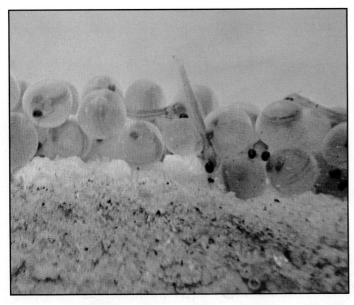

Most fish are born from eggs. Most fish do not take care of their young. How are fish different from birds and mammals?

Fish are **cold-blooded**. Their bodies are not always warm. Fish that live in warm water have warm bodies. Fish that live in cold water have cold bodies.

All fish have **gills.** A fish uses its gills to breathe. The gills take air from the water. The gills are behind the slits on the side of a fish's head.

ACTIVITY

What to do

A. Look at a fish with a hand lens.

B. Draw what you see.

What do you see?

1. Tell how the scales look.

2. Find the gills. What do they look like? How do they feel?

3. Find the fins. What do they look and feel like?

What do you think?

4. How do scales protect a fish?

5. How do gills help the fish breathe?

6. How do fins help fish move?

PEOPLE AND SCIENCE

This person is a doctor for animals. An animal doctor takes care of many kinds of animals. The animals cannot tell the doctor how they feel. The doctor uses her eyes, ears, nose, and hands to check each animal. The doctor knows what each kind of animal needs to stay healthy.

Something Fishy
Down on the Farm

Many people like to eat fish. People have fished for thousands of years. They caught fish in oceans, rivers, lakes, and streams. Now scientists have found a way to grow fish on farms.

Farms for raising fish are called hatcheries. Machines on the farms keep fish eggs warm until they hatch. Other machines keep the water at just the right temperature after the eggs have hatched.

The fish are taken care of until they are big enough to sell. These fish are fed special foods. This makes them grow faster and larger.

Some of the fish you eat may have been raised in hatcheries. Catfish, salmon, and trout are some of the fish that are raised in hatcheries.

What Do You Think?

Give two reasons why you think fish hatcheries are a good idea.

Chapter Review

Main Ideas

- Mammals are warm-blooded animals with hair.

- Birds are warm-blooded animals with feathers.

- Fish are cold-blooded animals that live in the water and have gills.

Science Words

Match each word with the same part in the picture.

mammal fins   wings
feathers bird   hair
beak   fish   gills
scales

Questions

1. Mammals breathe air with their _____ .

2. Fish use their _____ to breathe.

3. What body parts help fish live in water?

4. Look at these pictures. Group the animals—mammal, bird, or fish.

5. Which ones are warm-blooded?

Chapter 2

More Animal Groups

1.
REPTILES

Snakes, lizards, and turtles are
reptiles. Reptiles are covered with scales.
Their skin may feel rough and dry.

All reptiles are cold-blooded. When
the air is warm, a reptile feels warm.
When it is cold outside, their bodies
are cold. If a reptile is cold, it cannot
move fast.

Most reptiles lay eggs. The eggs are laid on the land. The babies hatch from the eggs. The parents do not feed their babies. How do you think the babies get food?

Many reptiles can swim. They do not breathe under water. Reptiles breathe air with their lungs.

Many reptiles are the same color as the things around them. Can you find the reptile in the picture? How does its color help it?

Some reptiles use their tongues to help them smell.

Some reptiles shed their skin as they grow. This lizard is shedding its skin. There is new skin under the old skin.

Reptiles live in forests, jungles, and
deserts. What reptiles live near you?

Crocodiles and alligators are reptiles, too.
How are these two reptiles the same?

What to do

A. Look for reptiles in an animal book.

B. Make a list of all the reptiles you find.

C. Put the reptiles into groups. What are the names of your groups?

What do you see?

1. How are the reptiles in each group the same?

What do you think?

2. Tell another way to group reptiles.

2.

AMPHIBIANS

These salamanders are **amphibians.**
Amphibians are cold-blooded animals. Most
of them have wet, smooth skin. They have
no hair or scales. How are amphibians
different from reptiles?

A frog is an amphibian.

A toad is an amphibian, too. When
amphibians are young, they live underwater.
When they are older, they live on
the land.

Amphibians lay eggs in water.
Many eggs are laid together.

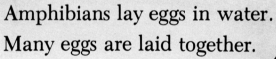

The eggs do not have hard shells.
The babies hatch from the eggs.

The babies breathe and grow in water. They have gills like fish. They can swim like fish. Baby amphibians find food underwater.

Baby amphibians are **tadpoles**. A tadpole begins to look more like its parents as it gets older. It grows legs and lungs. Then it can live on the land.

ACTIVITY

How can you show a frog's life cycle?

What to do

A. Look at a book about frogs.

B. On different cards, draw each stage of a frog's life:

- egg
- young tadpole with tail
- tadpole with legs
- adult frog

C. Punch holes in the cards. Use string to hang them from a hanger.

What do you see?

1. In what order did you put your pictures?

What do you think?

2. What other amphibian life cycles could you draw?

3.

INSECTS

A grasshopper is an **insect**. All insects have six legs. Insects have three body parts. Can you see the body parts and legs? Most insects have four wings. The grasshopper's wings are folded down. Can you name other insects?

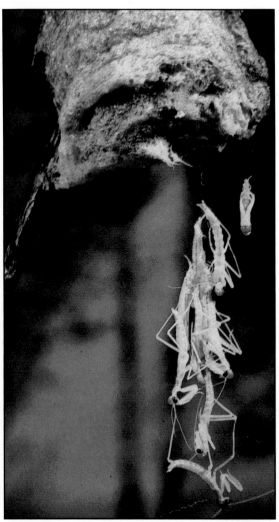

This is an adult praying mantis. It is an insect.

All insects lay eggs. Some baby insects look like their parents. These praying mantis babies just hatched. They are very tiny. But they look like their parents. Each baby has six legs. Each baby has three body parts.

Some baby insects do not look like their parents. This is an egg laid by a butterfly.

The baby that hatches is called a **caterpillar.** The caterpillar eats and grows.

Soon it stops eating. It stays very still. It changes into a **pupa.**

Inside the pupa the insect is changing. **A** grown-up butterfly climbs out.

ACTIVITY
How does an insect move and eat?

What to do

A. Look for insects on plants.

B. Put an insect in a jar.

C. Add some green leaves from the same plant.

D. Cover the jar with a thin cloth.

E. Watch the insect.

F. Draw the insect.

What do you see?

1. How many legs does it have?

2. How does the insect move?

3. How does it eat?

What do you think?

4. How can you tell if an animal is an insect?

4.

ANIMALS OF LONG AGO

The earth is always changing. Long ago it looked very different. The animals of long ago were different, too. How do we know? People find **fossils.** Fossils are made of rock. Some fossils have footprints in them. Other fossils show the shapes of animals.

These bones are fossils, too. The bones came from an animal of long ago. They took many years to change to rock. The bones are very big. They came from an animal that is no longer alive. This animal is called a **dinosaur.**

Dinosaurs were reptiles. They laid
eggs on land. Some dinosaurs had scales
on their skin. Some dinosaurs were as
small as a chicken. These two animals
were very big. They could look over the
top of a house!

Not all animals of long ago were
reptiles. What kinds of animals were
these? One looks like a reptile. But it
had feathers and could fly.

Mammals also lived long ago. Which
animal looks like a mammal? What
animal of today does it look like?

These people are looking for dinosaur fossils. They dig them out of the ground. They hope to find all the bones of the animal.

The bones are taken to a museum. The bones are like the pieces of a puzzle. They fit together to make a skeleton. People visit the museum to see the skeleton.

HOW YOU LOOK FOR DIFFERENCES

Things are different in many ways. You can use your senses to **observe** differences.

You know that dinosaurs were many sizes and shapes. Dinosaurs were also different in another way. Look at the teeth on these dinosaurs. What differences do you observe?

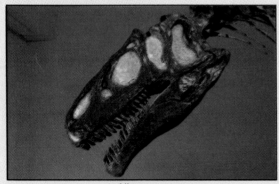

Allosaurus

Diplodocus

The dinosaur on the left had pointed teeth. Its teeth were good for eating meat. The dinosaur on the right had flat teeth. Its teeth were good for eating plants. All dinosaurs had teeth. The teeth on each dinosaur were different.

PRACTICE YOUR SKILLS

Use the pictures to find differences.

Triceratops

Stegosaurus

Iguanodon

1. Find differences in the heads of these dinosaurs.

2. Find differences in their bodies.

3. Find differences in how they moved.

USE YOUR SKILLS

Find pictures of birds. What differences do you observe?

Main Ideas

- Reptiles are cold-blooded animals with dry, rough skin.

- Amphibians are animals that live in water and on land.

- Insects are animals that have six legs and three body parts.

- Some animals that lived long ago do not live today.

Science Words

Match each word with a picture.

amphibian fossil reptile

dinosaur   insect tadpole

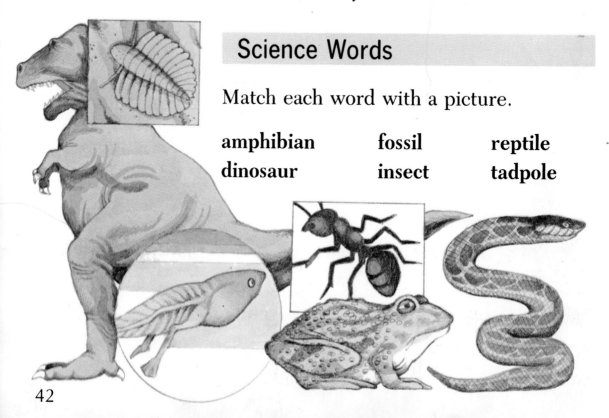

Questions

1. How are these two animals the same?

2. How are they different?

3. How does this insect grow up? Tell the right order of the pictures.

Science Project

Visit a library or museum. Find out about the earth long ago. What did plants look like? What kinds of animals were there? Draw how they looked.

You know that words in a dictionary are in alphabetical order. These words are in alphabetical order.

f *e* ather   f *i* sh   f *o* ssil   f *u* r

The first letter in each word is the same. When the first letter is the same, you use the second letter to put the words in alphabetical order.

Look at the words in the lists below. Put the words in each list in alphabetical order.

mother	**babies**	**smooth**
milk	**bird**	**swim**
meat	**beak**	**scales**
mammal	**bodies**	**snake**

In Chapter 1, you learned about three animal groups. The groups are mammals, birds, and fish.

Look at the pictures on pages 4, 8, and 12.

1. How are these animals alike?

2. How are these animals different?

In Chapter 2, you learned about reptiles, amphibians, and insects.

Look at page 37.

3. In which animal group do these dinosaurs belong?

4. Tell how scientists learn about the animals of long ago.

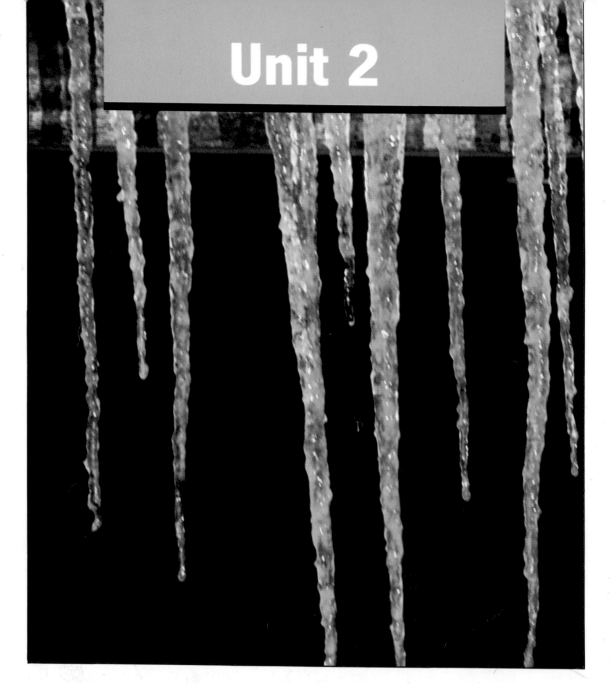

Unit 2

When water freezes, it turns to ice.

Look at the ice in this picture.

In what season do you think the picture was taken?

LOOKING AHEAD

Look at the pictures in this unit.

Find a tool used to measure temperature.

What is it called?

This picture shows a girl in the rain.

The rain is falling from the clouds.

Why don't the water drops stay in the air?

Chapter 3

Weather

1.

WHAT MAKES WEATHER?

Look out your window. What does the sky look like? Is the wind blowing? Is the air cool or warm? What is the **weather**? Sun, air, and water make the weather.

Look at the picture. The sun is
shining. It is a sunny day. Is the weather
warm or cold? How can you tell?

Moving air is called **wind**. The wind
can move things. Look at the sails on
the boat. The wind pushes them. Which
direction is the wind coming from?

The sky is covered with **clouds.**
The sun is behind the clouds. The sun
cannot be seen. It is a cloudy day.

Have you ever walked through a
cloud? A low cloud near the ground is
called **fog.** What kind of day is it in
this picture?

Rain falls from the clouds. What does it look like outside on a rainy day?

Snow falls from clouds. It piles up on the ground. It is cold outside. When the weather gets warm, snow melts. What can you do with snow?

What to do

A. Draw pictures showing different kinds of weather.

B. Guess what the weather will be like tomorrow. Put a picture of it on a chart.

C. Tomorrow, put a picture under it to show what the weather was really like.

D. Do this each day for one week.

What do you see?

1. Did the weather change?

2. Did you make good guesses?

What do you think?

3. Tell how you know what guesses to make.

2.

HOT AND COLD

The air around us can be warm or
cool. In the morning the air feels cool.
The children wear jackets and sweaters.

In the afternoon the air is warmer.
How are the children dressed? What
made the air warm? The sun warms the
air during the day.

The sun **heats** the earth. It heats the land and water. It makes the air warm, too. At night we have no sunlight. The night air is cooler.

Temperature tells you how hot or cold something is. It is important to know the air temperature. Do you know why?

We measure temperature by using a **thermometer.** The liquid inside the thermometer moves up as the temperature gets hotter. Look at this thermometer. Is the temperature hot or cold?

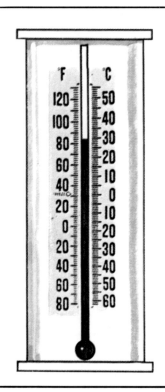

The liquid inside the thermometer moves down as the temperature gets colder. Look at this thermometer. Is the temperature hot or cold?

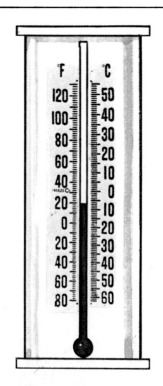

What to do

A. Fill one bowl with ice.

B. Fill another bowl with warm water.

C. Put a thermometer in each bowl.

D. Watch what happens to the liquid in each thermometer.

What do you see?

1. What number did the liquid in each thermometer reach?

What do you think?

2. What do you think the temperature might be on a cold day?

3. What do you think it might be on a hot day?

3.

THE SEASONS

Weather changes from day to day. It changes from **season** to season. It is hot in the summer and cold in the winter. It may be dry in the summer and rainy in the winter.

Weather changes make living things change. How does the weather change the things you do?

Plants change as the weather and seasons change. The leaves of some plants change color in the fall.

Some plants lose their leaves in the winter.

The weather changes in the spring. The air gets warmer. Many plants grow flowers in the spring.

Animals do different things as the weather changes. In the winter, some animals move to places where the weather is warm.

Many animals have babies in the spring.

In the winter, the daytime is shorter than the nighttime. It gets dark in the afternoon. In places where it is cold, people wear heavy clothes to keep themselves warm.

In the summer, daytime is longer than nighttime. The sun feels very hot. People wear light clothes to keep themselves cool in the summer.

ACTIVITY

In what weather do seeds grow best?

What to do

A. Put a wet towel in each of 2 dishes.

B. Put some seeds on the towels.

C. Cover the seeds with another wet towel.

D. Put one dish in a warm place. Put the other dish in a cool place.

E. Check your seeds every day. Keep the towels wet.

What do you see?

1. Which seeds grew faster?

What do you think?

2. Tell what weather is best for growing seeds.

PEOPLE AND SCIENCE

Weather is important to people who fly airplanes. An air traffic controller tells the pilots if it is safe to fly.

If there is too much rain, fog, snow, or wind, the planes may not fly. The air traffic controllers have machines that help them. Their machines tell them if storms are near.

HOW YOU GROUP THINGS

Things that are alike can be put in groups. When you group things, you **classify** them.

You know that the weather changes from season to season. It can also change from place to place. You wear different kinds of clothes for different kinds of weather.

Both of these children are going on a trip. Each of them is grouping, or classifying, their clothes for a different kind of weather.

The girl is going where the weather is hot. She is packing light, cool clothes. The boy is going where the weather is cold. He is packing heavy, warm clothes.

PRACTICE YOUR SKILLS

Use these pictures to answer the questions below.

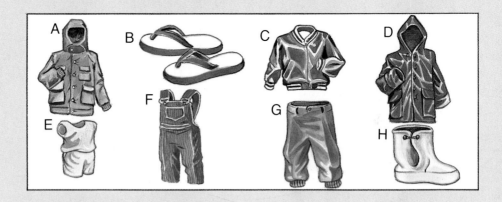

1. Which clothes would you wear on a hot summer day?

2. Which clothes would you wear on a rainy spring day?

3. Which clothes would you wear on a cool fall day?

4. Which clothes would you wear on a cold winter day?

USE YOUR SKILLS

Look at the pictures above. Find another way, besides the weather, to group, or classify, these clothes.

Main Ideas

- Sun, air, and water make the weather.

- Thermometers are used to measure how hot or cold it is.

- Weather changes from season to season.

- People, plants, and animals change as the weather changes.

Science Words

Pick the word that fits best in each blank.

| snow | seasons | rain |
| wind | thermometer | fog |

1. A _____ tells us the temperature.

2. _____ is moving air.

3. Low clouds near the ground are _____.

4. Summer and winter are two _____ .

5. _____ falls from clouds as white flakes.

6. _____ is water that falls from clouds.

Questions

1. Look at the picture.
   What is the weather?

2. How will the tree
   look in winter?

3. Which thermometer shows a
   hot day?
   Which thermometer shows a
   cold day?

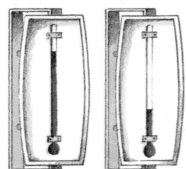

Science Project

Find out how much rain falls. Get a clear jar with straight sides. Put a ruler on the side. Put the jar outside. After it rains, look at the jar. How much water is in it?

Chapter 4

Water in the Air

1.

WHAT IS AIR?

Air is all around our earth. We call air a **gas.** It is the gas that we breathe. We need air to live. We cannot see, smell, or taste air. What can you see in the air?

The air around the earth is always moving. Wind is air on the move. Wind can push things. Sometimes the wind is very strong. Sometimes the wind is weak. Watch the clouds on a windy day. The wind pushes them.

We feel changes in the air. The air can feel warm or cool. The air can feel clean and dry.

Sometimes the air feels wet. It makes our skin feel sticky. Wet air makes you feel hot. How does the air feel here? Is it warm or cool? Is it dry or wet?

What to do

A. Look outside. See what the wind is able to move.

B. Look at the chart. Find the kind of wind there is today.

C. Check the wind again later in the day.

What do you see?

1. How strong was the wind today?

2. Did it change?

What do you think?

3. How strong do you think the wind will be tomorrow?

Name of wind	What you can see
Calm	Leaves on trees are still. Smoke rises straight up.
Gentle Breeze	Leaves moving. Wind moves flag a bit.
Strong Breeze	Large branches are moving. Umbrellas are hard to use.
Gale	Twigs snap off trees. Hard to walk.

2.

WHERE DOES WATER GO?

Oh! What fun! It has just rained. The children are playing in rain puddles. The sun is shining on the puddles. Soon the puddles will be gone. Where does the water go?

Heat helps make water go into the air. Where did heat come from to dry up the ground?

The wind helps make the water go into the air, too. What is helping to dry these clothes? Where does the water go?

Water that is in the air is called **water vapor.** What is making water change to water vapor? Water goes into the air in many places. Can you name some of these places?

ACTIVITY   What happens to water?

What to do

A. Fill some jars with water.

B. Mark the top of the water.

C. Put the jars in different places in the room.

D. Look at the jars in 2 or 3 days.

What do you see?

1. Did the level of the water change in any of the jars?

2. Did the water change by the same amount in every jar?

What do you think?

3. Tell why the level of the water changed.

3.

WHERE DOES WATER COME FROM?

We cannot always see water vapor. But it is always in the air. Water vapor can change back into water. Have you ever seen water on plants in the morning? The cool night air changed water vapor back to water. This water is called **dew**.

The sun shines on the plants. Soon the dew is gone. Where did it go?

The air is very cold high above the earth. In cold air the water vapor changes into drops of water. The drops of water and dust in the air make **clouds.**

The cloud drops get bigger and bigger. The drops of water get too heavy to float in the air. Soon they begin to fall. Then we have rain.

1. Heat from the sun changes water into water vapor.

2. The water vapor goes into the air.

3. Cold air changes water vapor back to drops of water.

4. The drops of water mix with dust to make clouds. What do you think will happen next?

What to do

A. Fill a glass with ice water.

B. Fill another glass with warm water.

C. Let the glasses sit for a few minutes.

D. Feel the outside of both glasses.

What do you see?

1. How do the sides of the glasses feel?

What do you think?

2. Tell why they are different.

4.

CLOUDS

There are many kinds of clouds. Their shapes, colors, and sizes are different. Clouds help us know what the weather will be.

These clouds are very big. They cover the sky. They look dark because they are made of many water drops. They are rain clouds.

These clouds look like cotton balls.
They seem to be always moving and
changing shape. The sun peeks through
these clouds.

When the clouds look like this, the
weather will be good. How are these
clouds different from rain clouds?

You can see these clouds on a clear, sunny day. They are the highest clouds in the sky. They are so thin you can almost see through them. They look like feathers in the sky.

The air is very cold high in the sky. These clouds are made of bits of ice.

What to do

A. Look at the clouds in these pictures. Tell how they are alike. Tell how they are different.

B. Look out the window. See if you can find clouds that look like any of the clouds in the pictures.

C. Draw a picture of the clouds each day for one week. On each picture, write what the weather was like.

What do you see?

1. Were the clouds the same each day?

2. What was the weather like? Was the weather the same each day?

What do you think?

3. How do clouds tell us about the weather?

PEOPLE AND SCIENCE

In some places the air gets very cold. The water vapor changes to ice. Ice in the air is called snow. It's fun to ski on snow.

Sometimes not enough snow falls. This person works a snow maker. The snow maker shoots tiny drops of water into the cold air. The water freezes and falls on the ground. The snow maker works all night to cover the ski slope.

Satellite Camera Takes Pictures of Clouds

Do you watch weather reports on TV? You may have seen pictures of clouds taken from a satellite. The satellite is high up in space. A camera on the satellite takes pictures of the weather back on earth. It takes a picture every 20 minutes. Each picture is different because the clouds are moving.

People who work in weather stations use these pictures. They put the cloud pictures together. Then, the pictures look like a movie. The moving pictures show which way the clouds are going. They also show how fast clouds are moving.

Satellite pictures also help us know what the weather will be like. The pictures from four different satellites can show us the whole earth at once. They can show us what kinds of clouds are moving towards us. Weather scientists can tell when it will be stormy or sunny.

What Do You Think?

Why do people want to know where clouds are going? Who might need to know what kinds of clouds are coming?

Chapter Review

Main Ideas

- The earth's air is always changing.

- Heat and wind change water into water vapor.

- Cool air changes water vapor into water.

- There are many kinds of clouds.

Science Words

The Science Words letters are mixed up. Write the words the right way.

1. Water in the air is *trwea pavro.*

2. Shapes in the sky made of water drops are called *olcdus.*

3. Drops of water on the ground in the morning are called *ewd.*

4. The sun's *teha* makes the water in puddles go into the air.

Questions

1. Which set of clothes will dry fastest?

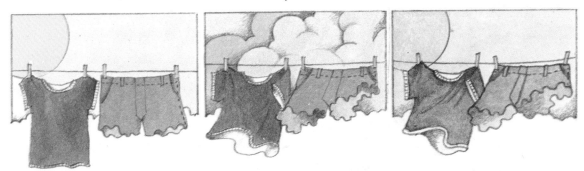

2. What are clouds made of?

3. What makes clouds move in the sky?

4. When you see feathery clouds you
   will have _____ weather.

5. What moves in the air that you like?

6. What moves in the air that is bad
   for you?

WORD STUDY

You know that two words can sound the same. Read the sentences below.

The sun went down. Mr. and Mrs. Hill's son went inside.

In these sentences, *sun* and *son* sound the same. Words that sound the same may have different spellings and have different meanings.

Read each pair of sentences below. Find the two words that sound the same. Tell what each word means.

1. Look at the sea. Do you see any fish?

2. The road was bumpy. I rode my bike carefully.

In Chapter 3, you learned about weather and how it changes.

Look at the pictures on pages 50, 51, and 52.

1. Tell about the weather in each picture.

2. What kind of clothes should people wear for each kind of weather shown?

3. How does each kind of weather affect what people, plants, and animals do?

In Chapter 4, you learned about water in the air.

Look at page 79.

4. What happens to water in the air?

5. Why is rain falling from the clouds?

6. Why does snow sometimes fall instead of rain?

Unit 3

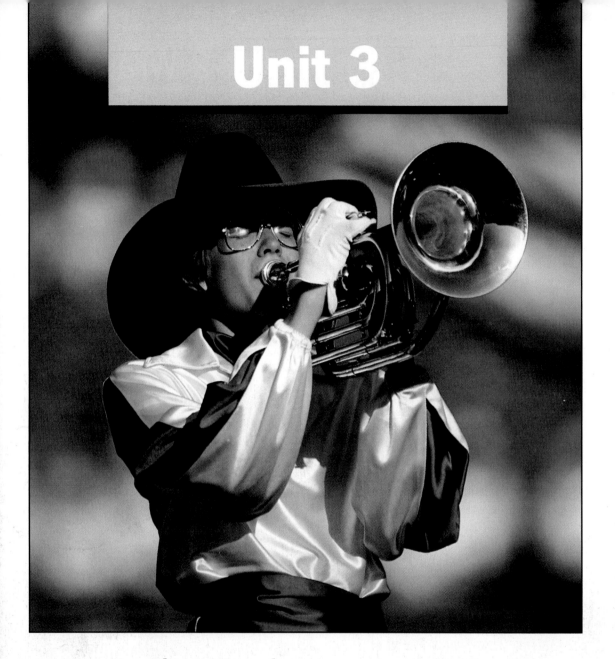

This picture shows a person playing an instrument.

He is using the instrument to make music.

What is the instrument made of?

LOOKING AHEAD

Look at the pictures in this unit.

Find one that shows a telephone you can make.

Tell how you would make it.

This lighthouse has a bright light.

Why does the light need to be bright?

Who does it help?

Chapter 5

Sound

1.

WHAT IS SOUND?

A **sound** is made when something moves back and forth very fast. When things move back and forth, they **vibrate.** What things in the picture are making sounds? The strings of the harp are vibrating. They move back and forth. They are making sounds.

This girl tapped a glass filled with water. Her tap made the glass, the water, and the air inside the glass move fast. This made a sound.

Tap on a desk. Do you see anything move back and forth fast? Sometimes things vibrate so fast that you do not see them move.

Sounds are made when air moves
back and forth fast. Blowing into a
bottle makes the air inside move fast.
The air vibrates. This makes a sound.

Blowing into a whistle makes sounds.
The air in the whistle vibrates. How are
these children making sounds?

What to do

A. Press half of a ruler down on a desktop.

B. Gently snap the end of the ruler that sticks out.

C. Then, snap it again harder.

D. Let more of the ruler stick out. Snap the ruler again.

What do you see?

1. How did the sound of the ruler change when you snapped it harder?

2. How did the sound change when more of the ruler stuck out?

What do you think?

3. Tell why the sound changed.

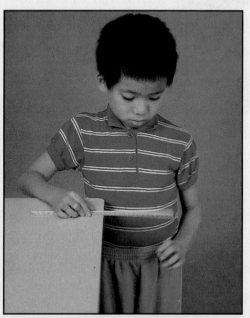

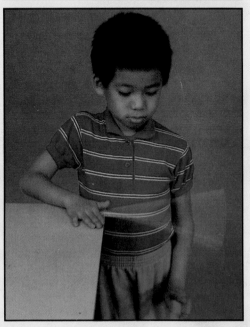

2.

SOUNDS ARE DIFFERENT

We know things by their sounds.
Sounds are different from each other.
Close your eyes. What sounds do you
hear? How are they different?

Some sounds are **high.** A whistle is a
high sound. What high sounds do you
know? Some sounds are **low.** A cow's
moo is a low sound. Can you think of
other low sounds?

Some sounds are
loud. A fire truck's
horn makes a loud
sound. Why is it
loud? What loud
sounds do you know?

Some sounds are
soft. A whisper is a
soft sound. What
soft sounds do you
know?

Some sounds are too loud for us. Very loud sounds can hurt our ears. What is making loud sounds here?

This worker is taking care of his ears. He wears a headset to block the loud noises. What other loud noises hurt your ears?

What to do

A. Put a rubber band around a ruler. Put a pencil under the rubber band.

B. Snap the rubber band gently. Then, snap it harder.

C. Move the pencil to different places on the ruler. Snap the rubber band. Listen to the sound each time.

What do you see?

1. When did the sound change?

What do you think?

2. Tell how you can make a louder or softer sound.

3. Tell how you can make a higher or lower sound.

3.

SOUND MAKERS

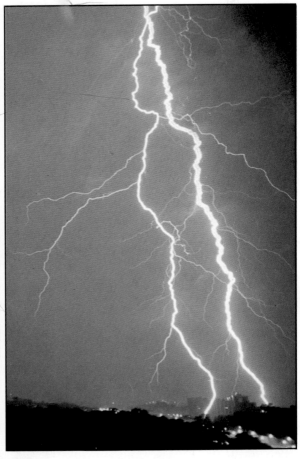

The world is full of sounds. Animals make sounds. A cricket vibrates its legs to make sound. Machines make sounds.

What sounds does the weather make? Raindrops, thunder, and wind make the sounds of a storm. Every time a sound is made, something vibrates.

Some sounds make music. What
things are these children using to make
music? What part of each music maker
vibrates?

Animals make many sounds. These
animals make sounds with their **throats.**
The air in the throat vibrates. The
vibrating air makes a sound.

What kind of sound does a kitten
make? Is it high or low?

Kittens and lions use their throats
to make sounds. In what other ways do
animals make sounds? How do you
make sounds?

What to do

A. Put your hand on your throat.

B. Hum softly. Then, hum louder.

C. Make other sounds with your throat.

D. List some words for the sounds you made. Describe how they feel.

What do you see?

1. What do you feel when you hum softly?

2. What do you feel when you hum louder?

3. What do you feel when you make other sounds?

What do you think?

4. What happens in your throat to make sounds?

4.

SOUNDS MOVE

Sounds can move. They move to our
ears. Sounds move through the air.
There is air between the teacher and the
students. The teacher's throat makes the
air vibrate. When air vibrates, small
parts inside your ear vibrate, too. Then
you hear the sound.

Sounds also move through objects.
One child makes a sound. The sound
makes the string move. The string
vibrates. Sounds move through the
string. The sound moves into the other
child's ear.

Sounds move through some things better than others. A boy is walking on a wood floor. The sound is loud.

The other boy is walking on a carpet. The sound is soft. Does sound move better through wood or carpet? How do you know?

What to do

A. Fill a bag with cotton.

B. Hold the bag next to your ear.

C. Have a friend hold a clock next to the bag.

D. Listen for the tick.

E. Try this again with a bag of air.

What did you see?

1. When was the sound louder?

What do you think?

2. Does sound travel better through cotton or air?

3. What other things is it hard for sound to travel through?

PEOPLE AND SCIENCE

Did you ever look inside a piano? Could you build one? That's what people in a piano factory do.

This person pulls steel wires across a metal frame. The wires are called strings. Piano strings must be very tight. The strings vibrate to make music.

Chip-Chat

People Use Computers to Make Music

Computers are used for many things. You can play games on computers. You can solve problems on computers. You can also write stories on computers. Now, you can even make music with computers.

Making music with a computer is fun. You can write your own song. Then, you can hear what it sounds like. It is easy and quick for just one person to make music. You do not need a different person to make each of the different sounds.

A computer can make sounds just like real musical instruments. It can make sounds like a guitar, drums, or a whole band. You can hear what your song will sound like played by any of these instruments. You can also change the sound of your song. Just push a button!

What Do You Think?

Will computers ever take the place of real musical instruments? Why or why not?

Chapter Review

Main Ideas

- A sound is made when something moves back and forth very fast.

- Sounds are high, low, loud, or soft.

- Sounds travel to our ears.

- Sounds travel better through some things than through others.

Science Words

Match each word with a picture.
Tell how each sounds.

high   **low**   **loud**   **soft**

Questions

1. Look at the picture. What will happen to the beans when the drum is hit?

2. What part of the drum vibrates?

3. What sounds can hurt your ears?

   high　　　**low**　　　**loud**　　　**soft**

4. How does your throat make sounds?

5. Why do some schools have carpet on the floors?

Science Project

Collect things that you can use in a band. Make up a beat for your instruments. Teach it to your friends.

Chapter 6

Light

1.

LIGHT MAKERS

Light comes from many things. The sun makes its own light. It is a giant ball of fire. The sun is a **bright** light.

A candle makes its own light. It is not a bright light. The candle's flame is small. It is a **dim** light.

We do not see the sun's light at night.
How do we see at night? People make
light bulbs to help us see. Light bulbs
make their own light.

Where are light bulbs used? Are they
bright or dim? What other things make
their own light?

We cannot see without light. Places
without light are very dark. You can't
see in the dark. A closet is dark. What
helps you see in a closet?

Do you like a light in your room
at night? How does it help you?

ACTIVITY

Do you need light to see things?

What to do

A. Tape a crayon inside one end of a shoe box.

B. Cut a small hole in the other end of the box. Put the lid on.

C. Roll up a piece of black paper. Fit it into the hole.

D. Look into the box. Lift the lid a little bit. Look again.

What do you see?

1. What did you see when the lid was closed?

2. What did you see when the lid was lifted?

What do you think?

3. Tell why you cannot see in the dark.

120

2.

HOW LIGHT MOVES

Light moves in a straight line. The sun's light moves through space. It hits only part of the earth at one time. The earth turns. Each part has light and then darkness.

When the sun's light shines, it is **day.** What do you do in the day? It is dark on the other side of the earth. We call this **night.** What do you do at night?

When light moves, it hits things
in its path. Light bounces off things
in straight lines.

The flashlight shines into a mirror.
The light **reflects** off the mirror. It
reflects in a straight line. Where does
the light move next?

Most things do not make their own light. We see these things when light reflects off of them. The light reflects into our eyes.

How do we see the actress? A light bulb makes the light. The light bounces off the actress. Then the light moves to our eyes.

What to do

A. Stand around the corner from a classmate.

B. Turn on a flashlight. Aim it straight ahead.

C. Ask another student if the light reaches the classmate.

D. Have the other student stand in the corner and hold a mirror.

E. See if the light will go around the corner.

What do you see?

1. Did the light reach your classmate with the use of the mirror?

2. Did it reach your classmate without the use of the mirror?

What do you think?

3. Tell what the mirror did to the light.

3.

LETTING LIGHT IN

These children are at the zoo. The clean glass makes it easy for them to see. Light moves through the glass easily. What do the children see through the glass? Where else do people use glass?

Sometimes the glass gets dirty. Then it is hard for light to move through it. The dirt on the glass blocks the light. Where else does glass get dirty?

What is over the ruler, scissors, and pencil? All light passes through them. We can see through these things.

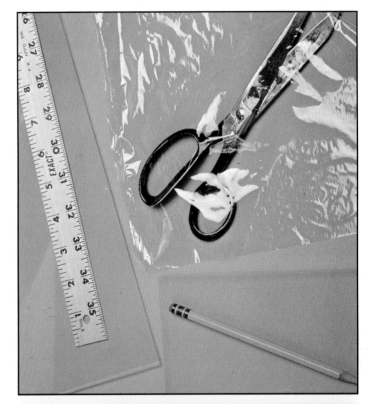

The ruler, scissors, and pencil are now harder to see. What is over them? Only some light passes through these things. We cannot see clearly through these things.

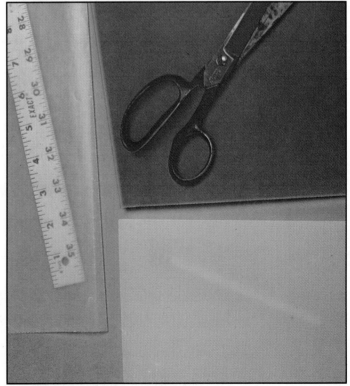

No light passes through these things. We cannot see through these things.

What things in this room let all light through? Which things let some light through? Which things let no light through?

ACTIVITY

What to do

A. Make a chart to show which things let light through.

B. Find 5 or 6 things to hold up to a light.

C. First, guess if the object will let light through. Then, hold it up to the light.

D. Write your answers on the chart.

What do you see?

1. Which things let light through?

2. Which things did not?

What do you think?

3. Tell when it is helpful to let light through.

4. Which things could be used as a window shade?

4.

SHADOWS

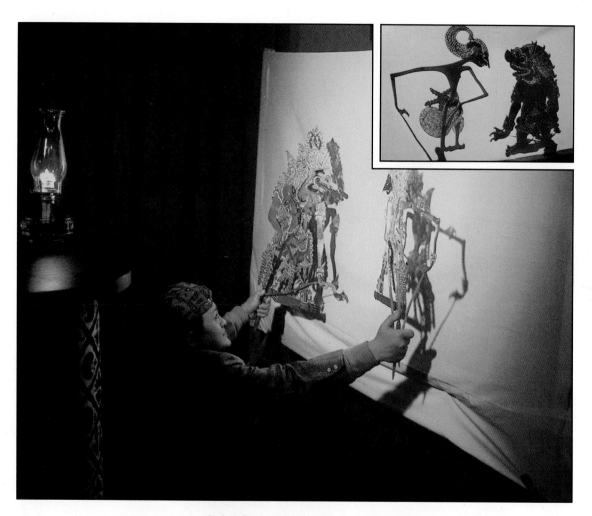

You need light to make a **shadow.**
The light can come from the sun. Or, it
can come from a lamp.

Something must block the light to
make a shadow. Look at the shadows in
the picture. What is blocking the light?

You make a shadow. Your body blocks
the light. Shadows can change. You can
move the light. The size of the shadow
will change. You can make your shadow
big or small.

Look at your shadow. Sometimes it looks the same as you. You can turn your body. The shape of your shadow will change. What kinds of shadow shapes can you make?

ACTIVITY

Do shadows made by the sun change?

What to do

A. Ask a classmate to trace your shadow in the morning sunlight.

B. Measure the length of your shadow.

C. Have your classmate trace your shadow at noontime. Measure it again.

What do you see?

1. How long was your shadow in the morning?

2. How long was it at noontime?

3. Did your shadow change in other ways?

What do you think?

4. What made your shadow change?

PEOPLE AND SCIENCE

People come to see plays here. This is a theater. Light is used in many ways here. This person moves the lights. A spotlight hits only one actor at a time.

The lights can be bright or dim. The color of the lights can change. Lights help make the play happy, sad, or scary.

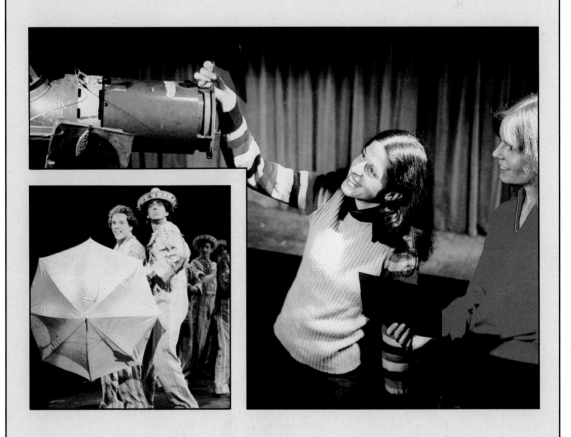

HOW YOU READ A GRAPH

You can find out things in different ways. One way to find things out is to read a graph.

You know that you need light to make a shadow. The light can come from the sun or from a lamp. If the light moves, the length of the shadow changes.

This graph tells you how long Mary's shadow is at different times. At 8 o'clock in the morning, her shadow is 80 centimeters long. At 9 o'clock in the morning, her shadow is only 60 centimeters long.

LENGTH OF MARY'S SHADOW	
8:00 A.M.	▢▢▢▢▢▢▢▢
9:00 A.M.	▢▢▢▢▢▢

Each ▢ stands for 10 centimeters.

PRACTICE YOUR SKILLS

This graph tells us what happens to Pat's shadow as the sun moves. Answer the questions below.

LENGTH OF PAT'S SHADOW	
9:00 A.M.	▢▢▢▢▢▢▢
10:00 A.M.	▢▢▢▢
11:00 A.M.	▢▢

Each ▢ stands for 10 centimeters.

1. How long is Pat's shadow at 10 A.M.?

2. At what time is Pat's shadow the longest?

3. At what time is Pat's shadow the shortest?

USE YOUR SKILLS

Make up another question about this graph. Ask a classmate to answer it.

Main Ideas

- We need light to see.

- Some things give off their own light.

- Light travels in a straight line.

- Light bounces off many things.

- Light travels through some things better than through others.

- Things that block the light make shadows.

Science Words

Pick the word that fits best in each blank.

day	**bright**	**light**
dim	**night**	

1. A _____ light makes a dim light.

2. We cannot see without _____.

3. The sun is a _____ light in the _____.

4. The light from a candle is very _____.

Questions

1. What things give off their own light?

2. Where is the boy's shadow?

3. Look at the objects. Which ones let all light pass through?

4. Which objects let a little light pass through?

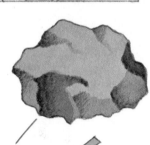

5. Which ones let no light pass through?

6. Which ones will make the darkest shadows?

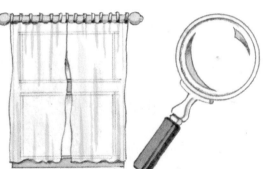

You know that light can be bright or dim. The words *bright* and *dim* have opposite meanings. What is the opposite of *loud?*

The word pairs below are opposites. Some words are missing. Copy the sentences onto another sheet of paper. Fill in each blank. Use a word from the box. When you have finished, each two lines should rhyme. The first one has been done for you.

night
low
sad
light
soft

Good and bad,

Happy and <u>sad</u>.

Fast and slow,

High and _____.

Dark and _____,

Day and _____.

Which word pair describes sounds?

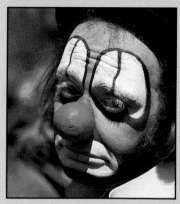

In Chapter 5, you learned about sound.

Look at pages 107, 108, and 109.

1. How do sounds travel?

2. Draw a picture showing how sound travels from a friend's mouth to your ear. Explain your picture to someone.

In Chapter 6, you learned about light.

Look at the picture on page 122.

3. Tell what would happen if the woman put her hand in front of the flashlight.

4. What would happen if the girl on the right held the mirror over her head?

5. What would happen if the girl on the left put the clock on the floor?

Unit 4

This snowplow is powerful.

It uses a lot of force.

How does it move the snow?

140

LOOKING AHEAD

Look at the pictures in this unit.

Which ones show people moving?

Who do you think is moving quickly?

Sliding is fun.

You can move very fast.

What makes you move easily down a slide?

Chapter 7

Force

1.

WHAT IS A FORCE?

A weightlifter **pulls** the bar up from the floor. Then he **pushes** it above his head. People, machines, and animals can push or pull.

A motorboat is a machine. It can pull a person on waterskis. The boat pulls the man over the water.

143

A **force** is a push or a pull. What kind of force do you see here? What does this machine do?

The boy is using a force. What kind of force is it? What forces do you use when you play?

A **strong force** is a big push or pull.
This big engine is pulling the train. It
pulls with a strong force.

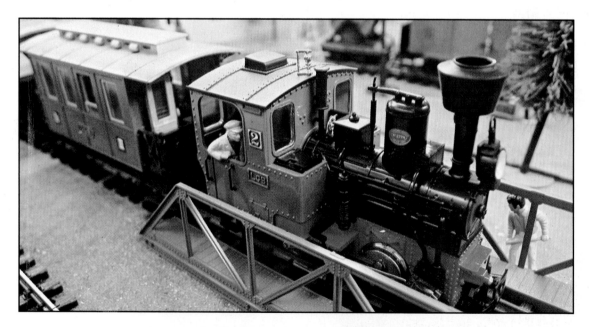

A **weak force** is a small push or pull.
This is a toy engine. It pulls with a
weak force.

ACTIVITY

Is the force a push or a pull?

What to do

A. Make a chart of things to move.

B. Move 5 things.

C. Mark on your chart which force you used, a push or a pull.

What We Moved	Push	Pull
door		

What do you see?

1. Which force did you use to move each thing?

2. Which force did you use the most?

What do you think?

3. Could you use a push or a pull to move each thing?

2.

FORCES MOVE THINGS

An elephant is hard to move. Many students are pulling. They use a lot of force. Will they be able to move the elephant?

Heavy things are hard to move.
Which wagon has a heavier load? How
do you know? A strong force is needed
to move heavy things.

A weak force is needed to move **light**
things. Which wagon do you think needs
less force to be moved?

The boy moves the weight up and down. When does he use more force?

Moving up a hill is harder than going down. Which child uses more force?

What to do

A. Make a ramp with a board and some books.

B. Tie one end of a string to a cup. Tie the other end to an object.

C. Place the object on the ramp. Let the cup hang off the ramp.

D. Put washers in the cup one by one. Stop when the object moves.

E. Take the washers out of the cup.

What do you see?

1. How many washers does it take to move the object uphill?

2. What happened when you took the washers out of the cup?

What do you think?

3. What did you do when you needed more force to move the object?

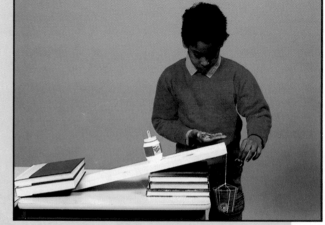

3.

FORCES CHANGE THINGS

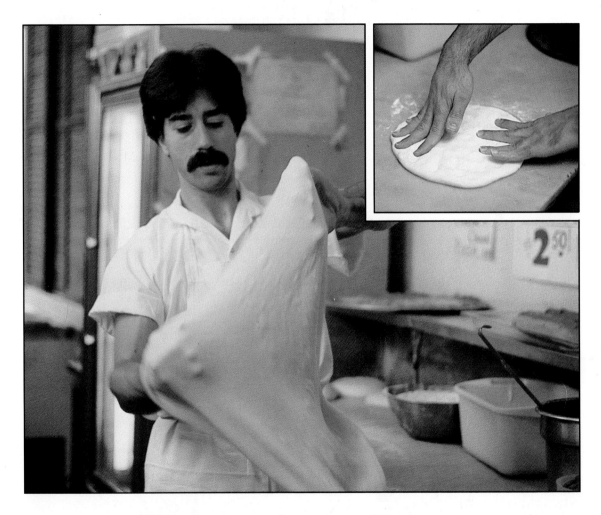

This person makes pizza. He gets a round piece of dough. The dough is pushed. It makes a flat **shape**.

Then the dough is pulled. Pulling changes the **size**. It gets bigger. Now it's ready for sauce and cheese!

Forces change the **speed** of things. How can the girl go **faster**? She pushes harder. She uses more force. The bike moves faster.

Forces can make things go **slower**. The dog wants to go fast. The boy pulls hard. He uses a strong force. The force makes the dog go slower.

Forces can change the **direction** things move in. The girl changed the direction of the ball. What kind of force did she use?

The truck turns a corner. It pulls its load along. It uses a force to change direction.

ACTIVITY

What forces do you use to change a shape?

What to do

A. Make a clay ball.

B. Press down on the ball with your hand.

C. Pull it with both hands.

D. Draw pictures to show how the shape of the clay changed.

What do you see?

1. How did the clay change shape when you pressed on it?

2. How did the clay change shape when you pulled on it?

What do you think?

3. Tell what forces you used to change the shape of the clay.

HOW MUCH FORCE?

These people are pushing carts in a store. The cart with more things is heavier. It takes more force to move it. Which person must push harder?

The horses are pulling loads of hay.
How many horses are pulling each load?
Two horses have more force than one.
Which load needs more force to move?
Which load **weighs** more?

The boy wants to lift the toys. He is pushing down on the seesaw. The toys are too heavy for him to move. They weigh a lot. What can he do?

Now a friend helps him. The force of two children can move the toys.

What to do

A. Set up a balance.

B. Put a ruler in side A.

C. Put paper clips in side B until the two sides balance.

D. Find how many paper clips you need to balance other things.

E. Order the things from lightest to heaviest.

What do you see?

1. Which thing needed the most paper clips to balance?

2. Which thing needed the fewest?

What do you think?

3. Tell whether it takes more force or less force to lift something heavy.

PEOPLE AND SCIENCE

Visiting a gym is fun. It is also good for your health. A gym has many machines for people to move. The machines make you work hard.

You use the force of your body to move the machine parts. You can pull or push on a bar with weights. Pushing and pulling make your muscles stronger.

HOW YOU MEASURE

You can **measure** things in different ways. You know that you can use a balance to measure the weights of things.

Look at this picture. There is a plant on one side of the balance. On the other side is one kilogram. One side of the balance is straight across from the other. The plant weighs exactly one kilogram.

PRACTICE YOUR SKILLS

Use these pictures to answer the questions below.

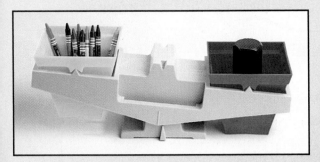 

1. Do the crayons weigh more than a kilogram?

2. Does the block of wood weigh less than a kilogram?

USE YOUR SKILLS

Look at these apples. About how many kilograms do you think they weigh?

Chapter Review

Main Ideas

- A force is a push or a pull.

- A force is needed to move things.

- A force can change the size and shape of things.

- A force can change the speed or direction of things.

- A force can be measured.

Science Words

Tell about the pictures.
Use these words.

pull	**weak**	**push**
strong	**heavy**	**light**

Questions

Find the picture that answers each question.

1. Which shows a change in direction?

2. Which shows a tool used to tell how much something weighs?

3. Which shows a change in the speed of a moving thing?

4. Which shows a weak force moving a light load?

Science Project

People, animals, and machines lift things. Find pictures of things being lifted. Is a push or a pull used to lift?

163

Chapter 8

Moving

1.

MOVING SLOWLY

Did you ever hike on a mountain path? Hiking can be hard work. These hikers are moving slowly. Their boots rub against the stones. The stones are slowing them down.

Moving on something **rough** slows
things. What is each child moving on?
Which child moves slower? Which child
needs more force to move?

When something moves, it rubs against other things. Rubbing slows moving things down. The truck's wheels rub against the dirt. The dirt is very rough. The dirt makes the truck move slowly.

You can throw a ball through the air. The ball rubs against the air. Air slows things down.

What to do

A. Push a block of wood over sandpaper.

B. Push the wood across a tile floor. Then push it across a carpet, a gym floor, and a sidewalk.

C. Make a list. Tell whether each surface is rough or smooth.

What do you see?

1. On which surfaces was it harder to push?

What do you think?

2. Tell what kinds of surfaces slow things down.

2.

SLOWING THINGS DOWN

Ice is very **smooth.** The ice skates move easily. Sometimes the skates move too fast.

This girl wants to stop. She turns and points her toe on the ice. Look at the toe of the skate. How will it help her stop?

169

Snow and ice make roads slippery.
Sand helps make the road rough. Sand
helps slow cars down.

Snow tires are very rough. They help
cars slow down without slipping.

Some shoes are made to help keep you from slipping. Their bottoms are rough. They help you slow down.

Look at the bottoms of these shoes. Which ones are for walking on snow? Which ones can grip wet grass? The white ones are for tennis. They let you slide a little bit.

What to do

A. Make a low ramp with a board and some books.

B. Put a toy truck at the top and let it go. Measure how far the truck traveled.

C. Put some sandpaper on the floor at the end of the ramp.

D. Put the truck at the top and let it go. Measure how far the truck traveled.

What do you see?

1. Which time did the truck travel farther?

What do you think?

2. Tell one reason why things move different distances.

3.

MOVING THINGS EASILY

Sometimes we want things to move faster and more easily. Things move faster and more easily on smooth things. The water slide is smooth. Are these people moving fast or slowly? Is it easy or hard for them to move? What would happen if the water were turned off?

The girl is putting oil on her toy. The oil makes the toy's parts slippery. The parts move smoothly against each other. This makes the toy move easily. What other things need oil to move easily?

Many things have
wheels. Wheels let
objects roll. Rolling is
easier than sliding.

Wheels make it
easier to move things.
You can move heavy
things with wheels.

ACTIVITY

What helps things move more easily?

What to do

A. Rub two fingers together.

B. Put some oil on your fingers. Rub your fingers together again.

C. Do the same thing with powder and sand. Clean your hands each time.

D. Make a chart. Show which ones feel rough and which ones feel smooth.

What do you see?

1. When was it easier to slide your fingers?

What do you think?

2. Tell which ones help things move more easily.

176

PEOPLE AND SCIENCE

Moving fast can save people's lives. Firefighters must get to a fire as fast as they can.

Many firehouses have a big pole. It joins the upstairs with the garage. The firefighters slide down the pole. The pole is very smooth. Sliding down is faster than walking on the stairs.

New Boat Travels Fast—It Hovers Above Water

Have you ever heard of a boat that travels on air? There is a new kind of boat that hovers just above the water. It is called a *hovercraft*.

A hovercraft touches the water at the start of a trip. It touches the water again at the end. In between, it doesn't touch the water. It travels just above the water. It floats on a cushion of air.

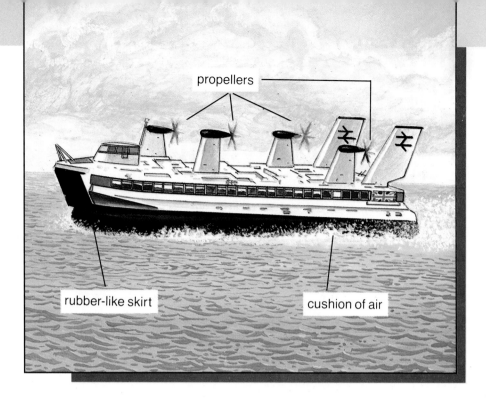

propellers

rubber-like skirt

cushion of air

There is a rubber-like skirt under and around the hovercraft. It looks like the inner tube of a large tire. The skirt holds air in place. Air is pumped under the boat to lift the boat off the water. Large propellers move it forward.

Water usually slows down a boat. A hovercraft can move fast because it doesn't touch water for very long. People use these boats to go across water quickly. People have also used them to travel across the frozen surface of Lake Erie.

What Do You Think?

In the future, how might "hovertrains" and "hovercars" change travel?

Main Ideas

- When something moves it rubs against other things.

- Moving over rough places slows things down.

- Smooth places make things move easily.

- Wheels and oil make things move easily.

Science Words

Look at the pictures.
Which show **rough** surfaces?
Which show **smooth** surfaces?

Answer the questions from the picture.

1. What makes the sled move easily?

2. What will make the sled slow down?

3. How could you stop the sled?

4. Will it take more force to go up or down the hill?

5. Will a sled go fast on a grassy hill?

6. How would a sled with wheels work on a grassy hill?

You can write about things that are happening now. You can also write about things that have already happened. Read the sentences below.

Today I lift the box. John lifted it yesterday.

The ending *-ed* is used to tell about something that has already happened.

Write two sentences using each of the words below. First, write about something that is happening now. Then, write about something that has already happened.

weigh   push   pull

In Chapter 7, you learned about force.

Look at pages 143, 144, and 145.

1. Find some pictures that show different forces.

    Find a force that pulls and a force that pushes.

    Find a weak force and a strong force.

2. Tell someone about your pictures.

    In Chapter 8, you learned about moving fast and moving slowly.

Look at the pictures on page 166.

3. What things help each skater move easily?

4. What things slow each skater down?

Unit 5

This man is fishing.

He is standing on a sandy beach.

Where does the sand on the beach
come from?

LOOKING AHEAD

Look at the pictures in this unit.

Find four animals that live in the ocean.

Which ones can you name?

Many different things live in the ocean.

What are some living things you can see here?

How are they different from things that live on land?

Chapter 9

Oceans and Beaches

1.

WHERE ARE OCEANS AND BEACHES?

The people are looking at a globe. A globe is a map of the **earth**. The blue parts on the globe show water. There is more water than land on earth. Some of the water is in **lakes** and **rivers**. Most of the water is in **oceans**.

Is there a **beach** near your home?
A beach is where the water meets the
land. The boy is standing on the beach.
Lakes, rivers, and oceans have beaches.

There are many kinds of beaches. They are made of different things.

There are rocky beaches.

There are sandy beaches.

Some beaches are made out of crushed shells.

ACTIVITY

Is there more water or land in your state?

What to do

A. Look at a map of your state.

B. Use colored clay to make a model of your state. Use brown clay for the land. Use blue clay for the water.

What do you see?

1. Where is there water in your state?

2. Is it in lakes or in rivers?

What do you think?

3. Is there more water or land in your state?

2.

HOW ARE BEACHES MADE?

There is sand in this lake. Water pushes the sand up onto the land. This makes a beach.

Shells are parts of sea animals. The shells are pushed onto the land by the water. This makes a beach.

Water is rubbing sand against these rocks. When this happens, the rocks will slowly break into sand.

The sand at this beach was made a long time ago from very large rocks. What helped change the rocks into the sand?

The wind blows sand against the
rocks. The wind and sand scrape the
rocks. Scraping changes the rocks into
sand. Wind and water work together to
help make beaches.

ACTIVITY

Where does sand come from?

What to do

A. Rub two rocks together over a paper towel.

B. Look at the paper towel.

What do you see?

1. What fell onto the paper towel?

2. How does it feel?

What do you think?

3. What made the pieces break off the rocks?

3.

OCEAN WATER

These people are sailing on the ocean. Water in the ocean is different from the water we drink. We cannot drink the ocean water. Ocean water is **salty**.

People drink **fresh water**. Fresh water does not have much salt in it. The water in lakes and rivers is fresh. The water we drink comes from lakes and rivers.

The water in
the ocean is always
moving. **Waves** are
made when the
wind moves water.

At certain times
each day, the ocean
water moves away
from the beach.
When this happens,
it is called **low tide**.

At other times
each day, the ocean
water moves closer
to the beach. When
this happens, it is
called **high tide**.

Small animals and plants live on the
beach. Walk on a beach at low tide.
Look near the rocks and puddles. You
can find ocean animals and plants. The
animals hold tight to the rocks.

ACTIVITY

How is salt water different from fresh water?

What to do

A. Look at some fresh water and smell it.

B. Take a sip of it to see how it tastes.

C. Mix a spoonful of salt in the water.

D. Find out how it looks, smells, and tastes now.

What do you see?

1. Does the salt water look, taste, or smell different from the fresh water?

What do you think?

2. What makes salt water different from fresh water?

4.

COLD AND WARM WATER

These people are divers. The ocean is
not **deep** here. It is **shallow**. The divers
are near the land. The water is warm
where the divers are. How do you know?

It is warm here. The sun is shining on
the top of the ocean. The water is warm.

Ocean water far from land is very
deep. The sun does not shine deep down
in the ocean. The water is very cold
here. The diver wears a suit to keep warm.

In warm parts of the world, the ocean water is warm. In cold parts of the world, the ocean water is cold.

Is the ocean water in the picture warm or cold? How do you know?

ACTIVITY

Whatpart of the ocean does the sun warm the most?

What to do

A. Fill a jar with cool water.

B. Find the temperature of the water at the bottom of the jar. Find the temperature near the top.

C. Shine a lamp on the water. Leave it on for about 30 minutes.

D. Take the temperatures again.

What do you see?

1. Were the temperatures the same or different in step B?

2. Did they change in step D?

What do you think?

3. Tell why the water near the top of the ocean is warmer than the water at the bottom.

Glass factories use a lot of sand. The sand is mixed with other materials. Then it is heated until it melts. A worker gathers the hot, glowing glass on a pipe.

The glassblower blows air into the pipe. A bubble is blown to make a bowl. Soon the glass cools. The glass bowl is then cut off.

HOW YOU PREDICT

You can often tell what will happen next. When you do this, you are **predicting.**

You know that water can be warm or cold. When water is very cold, it turns into ice.

This picture shows a river in winter. You can use what you know to tell what will happen to the ice in the spring.

In the spring, the days will be warmer. The heat from the sun will warm the water. The heat will melt the ice.

PRACTICE YOUR SKILLS

You know that the ocean has low and high tides. This picture shows a beach at low tide. Predict what will happen at high tide by answering the questions below.

1. What will happen to the water?

2. What will happen to the sand castle?

3. What will happen to the beach chair?

4. What will happen to the rocks near the water?

USE YOUR SKILLS

Look at the picture above. What do you think might happen to this beach in the winter? Tell why you think so.

Main Ideas

- Most water on earth is found in oceans.

- Beaches are found near water.

- Wind and water help make and change beaches.

- Ocean water can be warm or cold.

Science Words

Match each word to the right number on the picture.

river   ocean   lake
beach   earth   waves

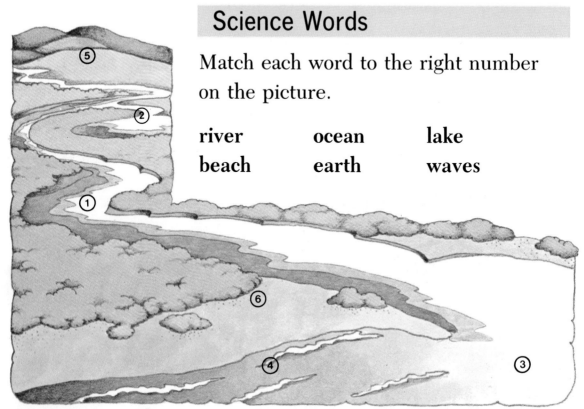

Questions

1. How are these made into beaches?

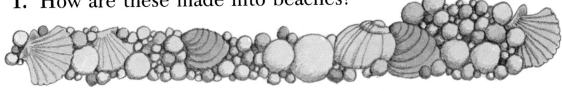

2. _____ pushes water to make waves.

3. How are ocean and lake water different?

4. Match the words with their pictures.

low tide   **high tide**

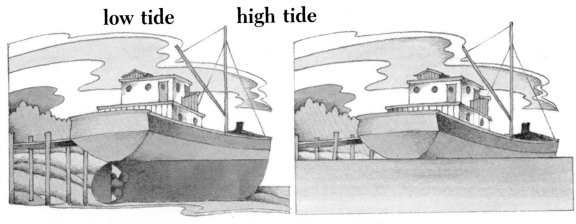

Science Project

Write to someone who lives near a beach. Ask him or her to send you a bit of the beach. Put it in a plastic bag. What is this beach made of?

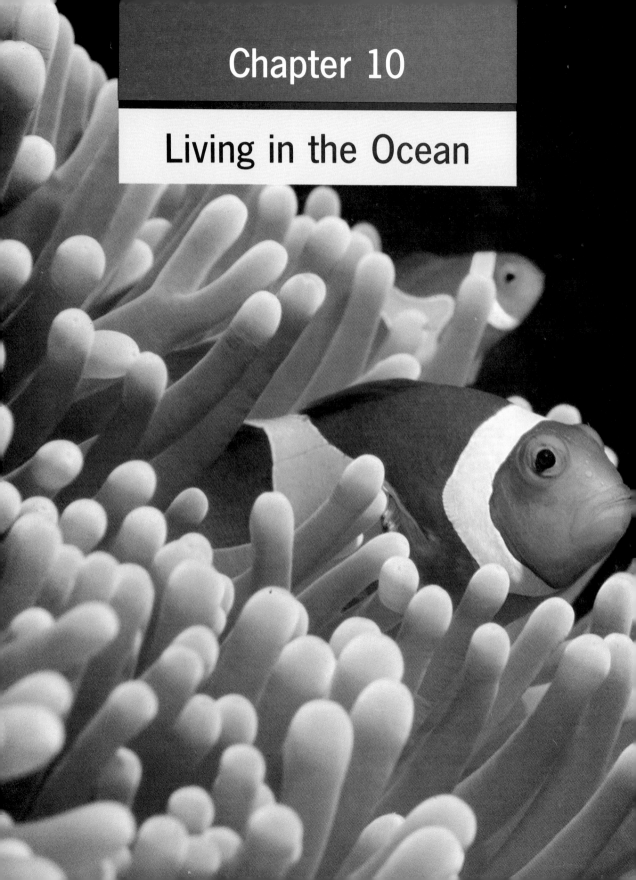

Chapter 10

Living in the Ocean

1.

OCEAN PLANTS

Ocean **plants** are different from land plants. Ocean plants can grow in salt water. Some ocean plants float in the water. Some hold tight onto rocks.

The waves push some of the plants onto beaches. These plants are many colors. What color are most land plants?

Most ocean plants need sunlight to
live. They grow only where they can get
sunlight. These plants grow in shallow
water. Can they grow in very deep water?

Many of the plants in the ocean are
very small. They float in the water.
They are so small you cannot see them
without a **microscope**. A microscope
makes things look bigger.

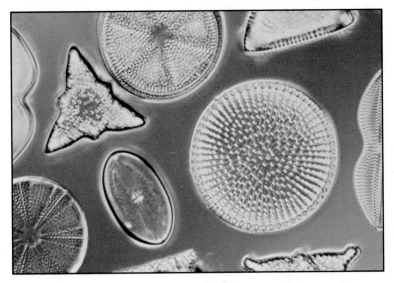

This is what
these small plants
look like through
a microscope.
What shapes do
you see?

ACTIVITY

How are water plants and land plants different?

What to do

A. Look at some water plants and some land plants.

B. Feel them and smell them.

C. Try to stand each one up.

What do you see?

1. Do the water plants and the land plants look the same?

2. Do they feel the same?

3. Do they smell the same?

What do you think?

4. How can you tell if a plant lives in the water or on land?

2.

OCEAN ANIMALS

Many kinds of **animals** live in the ocean. They move through the water in different ways. Some have smooth bodies. They swim in the water. Some animals have many legs. They crawl on the bottom.

The blue whale is the biggest animal
on earth. It is as long as three buses. It
lives in the ocean.

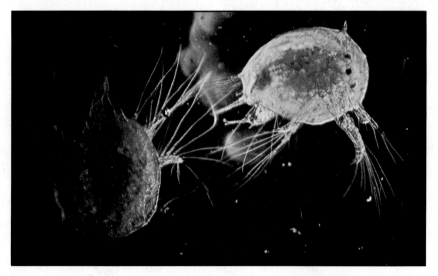

Some of the smallest animals live in
the ocean, too. These tiny animals eat
the small plants.

Look at the two pictures on this page. Are these plants or animals? They are ocean animals that look a lot like plants. They live on rocks at the ocean bottom.

These animals do not move from place to place. How can they find food? They wait for food to come to them. They trap bits of food that float in the water.

What to do

A. Look at some ocean animals from a fish market.

B. Draw a picture of each one.

C. Touch each one.

What do you see?

1. What do the animals look like?

2. How do they feel?

What do you think?

3. Tell how each animal moves.

4. Tell how they are different from land animals.

3.

FOOD IN THE OCEAN

All living things need food. Ocean plants use sunlight to make food. Some ocean animals eat plants. Some ocean animals eat other animals. Each living thing is food for another one. This is called a **food chain**.

Here is an ocean food chain.
Let's see how it is put together.

1. Tiny plants make their own food.
   They use sunlight to do it.

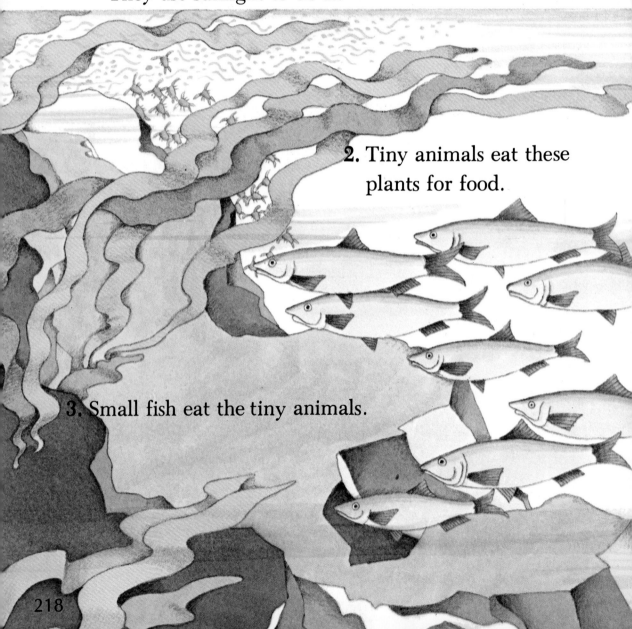

2. Tiny animals eat these
   plants for food.

3. Small fish eat the tiny animals.

5. People eat big fish for food.

4. Big fish eat the small fish.

What would happen to the big fish if
all the small fish were gone?

What to do

A. Find labels of things that are made from ocean animals.

B. Put the labels of things that are made from ocean animals on a piece of paper.

What do you see?

1. What are some of the things that are made from ocean animals?

What do you think?

2. Tell some of the ways that people use ocean animals.

PEOPLE AND SCIENCE

An aquarium is like a zoo. It is a place where people can see ocean animals. The animals live in tanks of salt water.

This person takes care of the animals. She knows what foods to give to each animal. She keeps the water at the right temperature. She knows what each animal needs to stay healthy.

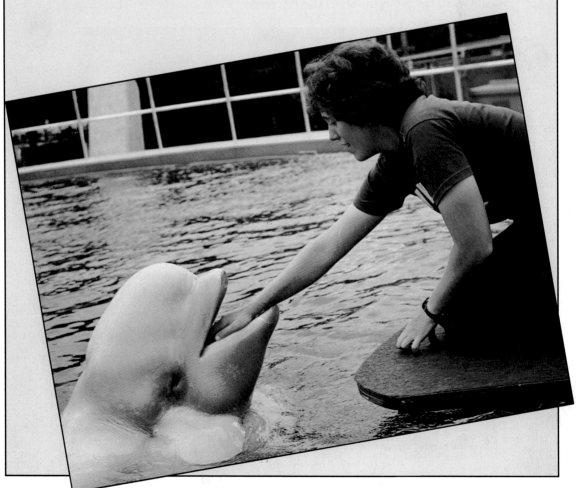

Floating Factories for Fish

A new kind of ship solves an old problem for people who fish. Fishing ships must sail into port often because fish spoils quickly. People who fish would like to stay at sea longer. This new ship helps them do that.

The new ships are floating factories. They are very big. More than 500 people can live and work on each ship.

People in smaller boats catch the fish. The smaller boats are called catcher boats. The catcher boats take the fish to a factory ship.

Workers on the factory ship can do the same things they can do on land. They use the latest machines on the ships. These machines clean, cut, cook, freeze, and can the fish. There is also a place on the ship to store the fish.

What Do You Think?

How do you think factory ships have helped people?

Main Ideas

- Ocean plants are different from land plants.

- There are many kinds of ocean animals.

- Ocean plants and animals need each other for food.

Science Words

Match each word with a picture.

microscope   **animal**
plant   **food chain**

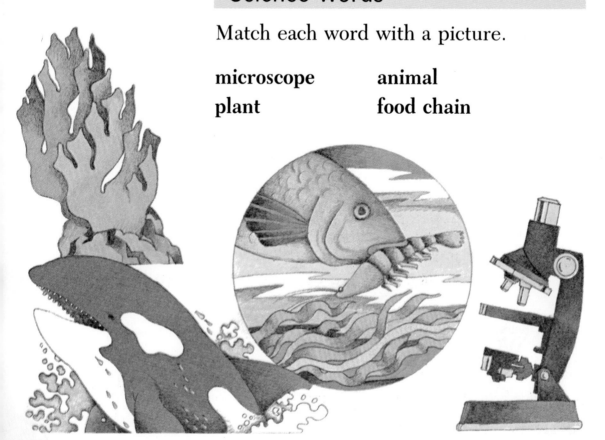

Questions

1. How are these plants different?

2. Name some ocean animals.

3. This food chain is mixed up. What is the right order?

Science Project

Make a shell collection. Group the shells by how they look. Show how the animal uses its shell.

WORD STUDY

The three fish are in order by size. The *tiny* one is first. The *small* one is next. The *big* fish is last. You can show the same order this way:

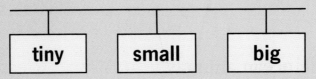

| tiny | small | big |

Warm and *cool* are temperature words. Copy the chart below. Put *warm* and *cool* in the right order on the line.

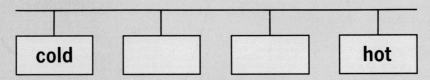

| cold | | | hot |

All these words are bodies of water.

lake   puddle   ocean   pond

A *puddle* is the smallest amount of water. Copy the chart below. Write the other words in size order. Put the biggest body of water last.

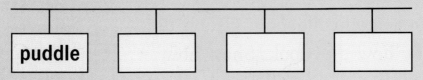

| puddle | | | |

In Chapter 9, you learned about oceans and beaches.

Look at pages 191, 192, and 193.

1. How are beaches made?

2. How do wind and ocean water work together to make a beach?

3. What would the water taste like at an ocean beach?

In Chapter 10, you learned about ocean plants and animals.

Look at the pictures on pages 218 and 219.

4. Why is this called a food chain?

5. How does the chain begin?

6. How does it end?

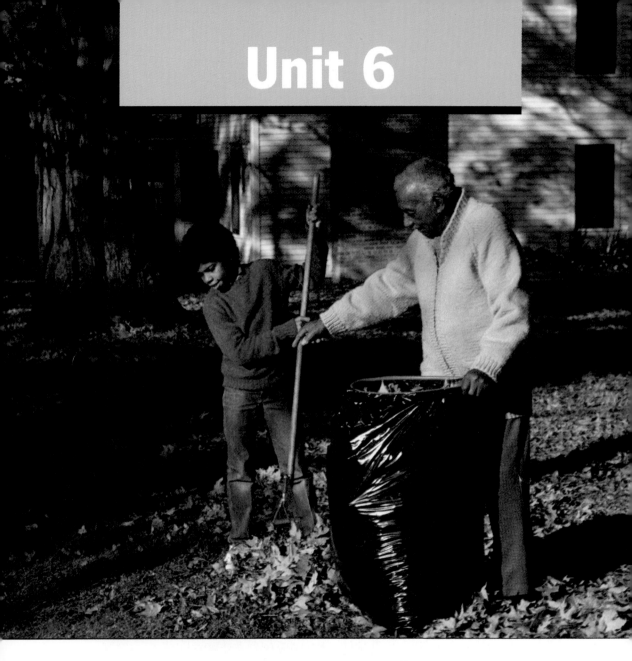

Leaves are an important part of a plant.

Where did these leaves come from?

Do you think they were always this color?

LOOKING AHEAD

Look at the pictures in this unit.

Which plants can you name?

Which plants can be eaten?

These plants are alive.

They are growing on a volcano.

What do you think they need to grow?

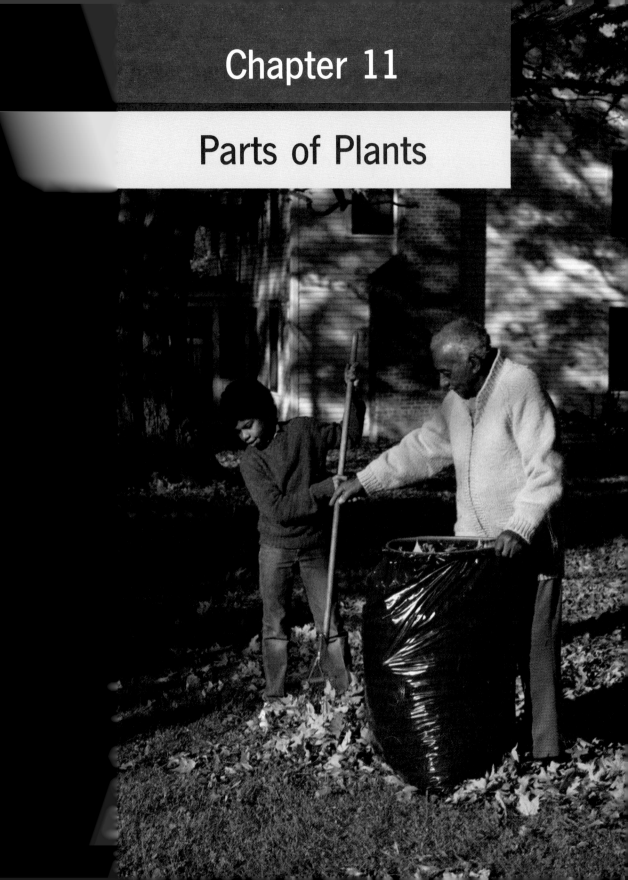

Chapter 11

Parts of Plants

1.

ROOTS

Many plants have **roots**. The root is the part that grows in the ground. Some plants have roots that grow underwater.

Roots are important to plants. The roots of a tree hold tight in the ground. They help the tree stand up. What would happen if the tree had no roots?

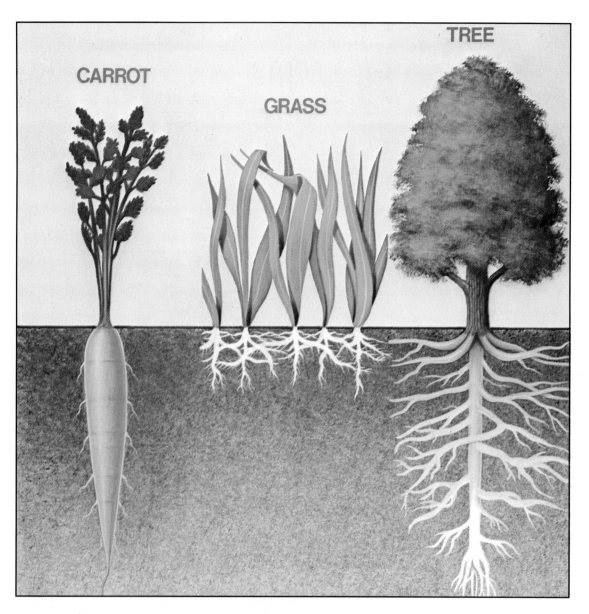

CARROT

GRASS

TREE

All plants use their roots to get water.
The water travels through the roots to
the rest of the plant.

Roots help the plant in other ways.
Some roots have very thick parts. The
plants store extra food in them.

We eat the roots of many plants. Do
you know the names of these foods?
They are all parts of roots.

What to do

A. Put toothpicks into the sides of a potato.

B. Put some water in a glass. Mix red food coloring in with the water.

C. Put the potato into this mixture.

D. Wait a few days. Cut the potato in half.

What do you see?

1. How did the potato change?

What do you think?

2. Tell why the potato changed.

STEMS

Stems are parts of plants. The stem is between the roots and the leaves. Wildflowers have soft stems. The trunk of a tree is a stem. Tree stems are hard and strong. What do people use tree stems for?

The stem helps the plant in two ways. The stem holds up the plant. It holds the leaves up to the sunlight.

Water moves up the stem. It travels from the roots to the leaves. Food moves down the stem. It comes from the leaves.

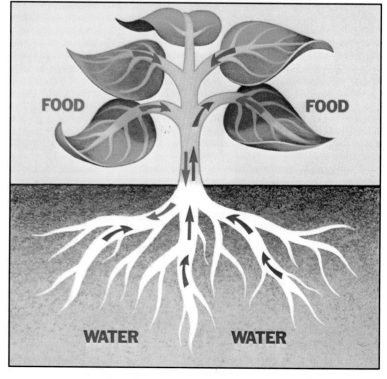

FOOD   FOOD

WATER   WATER

We eat the stems of many plants. Do
you know the names of these foods?
They are all stems of plants. What other
plant stems do you eat?

Stems grow under and above the ground.
The part above the ground is green.

How does water travel through a plant?

What to do

A. Mix red food coloring in some water.

B. Put a stalk of celery into the water.

C. Wait a day. Look at the leaves.

D. Cut off a piece of the stalk.

What do you see?

1. What happened to the leaves?

2. What did you see when you cut the stalk?

What do you think?

3. Tell how water travels to the leaves of a plant.

3.

THE LEAF

Each of these objects is a **leaf**. A leaf
is a part of a plant. The leaf grows on
the stem. How do they look the same?
How do they look different? All leaves
do the same job for plants.

The leaf makes food for the plant. It uses air, water, and sunlight. Water rises from the roots. Air comes in from tiny holes in the leaf.

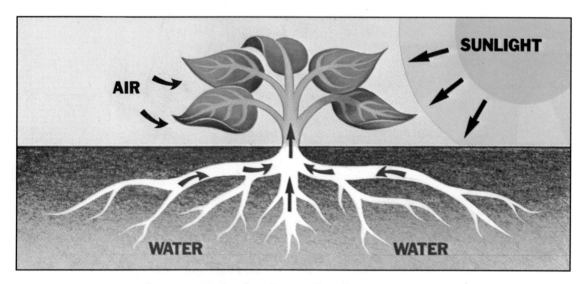

AIR

SUNLIGHT

WATER   WATER

The sun's light hits the leaves. Now the leaf can make food. Only green plants can make food.

Some leaves change color. They turn
from green to brown. The brown leaves
cannot make food. Soon the leaves drop
off the stems. Food is not made now. In
spring, new leaves grow. The leaves are
green. Can they make food now?

People eat the leaves of many plants.
These green leaves are very good for
you. Do you know the names of these
leaves? Which ones do you eat cooked?
Which ones do you eat raw? What other
plant leaves do you eat?

ACTIVITY

What to do

A. Put a plant on a piece of cardboard.

B. Put clear jelly around the rim of a large glass jar.

C. Put the jar over the plant. Write what you think will happen.

D. Wait a few days.

What do you see?

1. What happened to the inside of the jar?

What do you think?

2. Tell why this happened.

Petroleum Jelly

4.

FLOWERS AND SEEDS

Flowers for sale! Flowers for sale! People like flowers for their colors, shapes, and smells. **Flowers** are parts of plants. Not all plants have big, bright flowers. But all flowers have the same job. How do flowers help the plant?

A flower's job is to make **seeds**. This is the flower of a daisy. The seeds are made in the center of the flower. The seeds will fall to the ground. They will grow into new plants.

Each of these seeds will grow into a plant. Daisy seeds grow into daisy plants. Corn seeds can make only new corn plants. Seeds have different shapes, sizes, and colors.

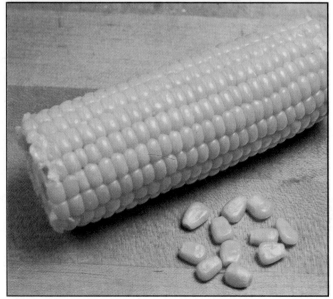

Some flowers make a cover for their seeds. The cover is called a **fruit**. Some fruits have many seeds inside. Other fruits have only one seed.

Many animals like to eat the fruits of plants. All of these are fruits. They all have seeds. Can you name the fruits? What fruits do you eat?

Some flowers make fruits that are hard and dry. These fruits also have seeds inside. These seeds are good to eat. They are peanuts.

An acorn is a hard, dry fruit. Inside the acorn is a seed. The seed will grow into an oak tree. What animals like to eat the seeds of oak trees?

What to do

A. Collect many kinds of seeds.

B. Dry them on paper towels.

C. Glue each kind of seed to a card. Write the name of the plant it comes from.

D. Put the seeds in groups.

What do you see?

1. How did you group the seeds?

2. What did you name each group?

What do you think?

3. Tell some of the differences between the seeds.

248

PEOPLE AND SCIENCE

Many people like to garden. Gardeners buy seeds to start their gardens. Where do the seeds come from?

The seeds are grown on special farms. The seed farmer picks the fruits when they are very ripe. The fruit is mashed up. Then the seeds are taken out and dried. They are put in packets and sold.

HOW YOU PUT THINGS IN ORDER

You can put many things in order. You know that living things grow. They grow in a special order.

These pictures show how a corn plant grows. The pictures are in order of time. The roots grow first. The stem and leaves grow next. Finally, there are new seeds.

PRACTICE YOUR SKILLS

The pictures below show how an oak tree grows. These pictures are not in order. First look at the pictures. Then answer the questions.

1. Which picture happened first?

2. Which picture happened second?

3. Which picture happened third?

USE YOUR SKILLS

Think about planting a garden. In what order would you do things? What would you do first? What would you do next? What would you do last?

Chapter Review

Main Ideas

- The roots, stem, leaves, and flowers are parts of plants.

- Each part has its own job.

- Seeds and fruits are made by the flowers.

- We eat many parts of plants.

Science Words

Match each word to a part of the plant.

fruit	**leaf**	**stem**
root	**flower**	**seeds**

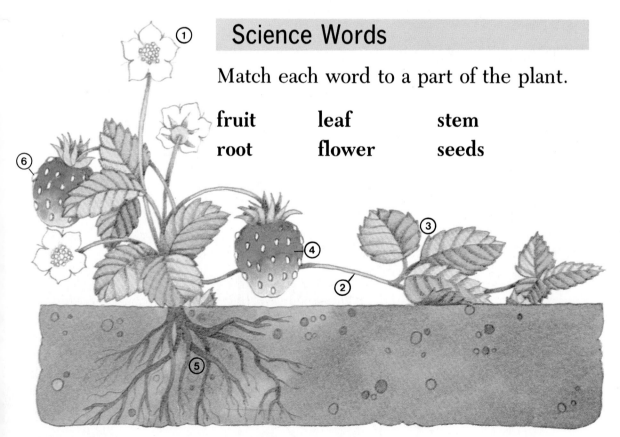

Questions

1. How does a plant get water?

2. Which tree here can make food?

3. What part of a plant makes seeds?

4. What do leaves use to make food?

5. Look at the picture. Which foods are leaves?

6. Which foods are roots?

7. Which foods are fruits?

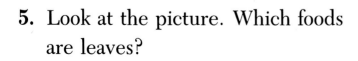
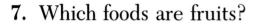

Chapter 12

Plants Are Living Things

1.

WHAT DO PLANTS NEED?

At this school the children work in a
greenhouse. A greenhouse is a place
where green plants grow. Green plants
are **living things**. The children learn
what green plants need to stay healthy.

All green plants
need sunlight to live.
The sunlight helps
green plants make food.

In what part of the
plant is food made?

Green plants need
air to live. Some green
plants live in water.
They use tiny bits of
air that are mixed in
with the water. The
air is used to make
food.

Green plants need water to live and
to grow. They use water to make food.
What happens to plants when there is
no water? How do they look?

Most green plants need soil to live.
Soil holds water for the plants to use.
The soil has bits of rock in it. The plant
uses the bits of rock to make its food.

What to do

A. Cover a leaf on a plant with black paper. The leaf will not get sunlight.

B. Cover another leaf with a plastic bag. This leaf will not get air.

C. Write down what you think will happen to each leaf.

D. Wait a week. Uncover the leaves.

What do you see?

1. How does each leaf look now?

What do you think?

2. Do plants need air? Tell why you think so.

3. Do they need sunlight? Tell why you think so.

2.

WHERE PLANTS GROW

A dandelion grows on a lawn. The yellow flower changes. It turns white and fluffy. The wind blows the seeds. Tiny hairs help them stay up in the air.

Soon a seed lands. If it falls on soil, it will grow. On what other places could it land? Would it grow there?

This maple seed was carried by the wind. It has a long wing. The wing helped it to fly. The seed landed on soil. There was some water in the soil. There was air around it. The seed started to grow into a tree.

Plants can grow indoors. The children give the plants soil, water, and light.

Some people grow plants around their homes. They plant grass seeds. They put whole plants in the soil.

What happens to soil when it rains?
These students are trying to find out.
Each tray of soil is like a hillside.

The roots of plants hold the soil.
When it rains, the soil stays in place.
Some hills have no plants. What
happens when it rains? People grow
plants on hills to hold the soil.

ACTIVITY

What to do

A. Put a paper towel in a cup.

B. Put a little water in the cup.

C. Place bean seeds between the paper and the cup.

D. Keep the towel damp. Watch the seeds change. Draw a picture of them every day.

What do you see?

1. Which part grows first?

What do you think?

2. What plant parts grow from seeds?

3.

IS IT A PLANT?

Around the trees are small, green plants called **moss**. Moss grows in damp, shady places. It grows in the forest. It can grow in the cracks of sidewalks.

Moss grows close together. Did you ever feel moss? It feels like a soft rug. Moss does not have flowers or seeds.

These living things are not green.
They cannot make their own food. They
grow on dead plants and animals. Others
grow on soil. They are called **fungi.**
Which kinds of fungi have you seen?

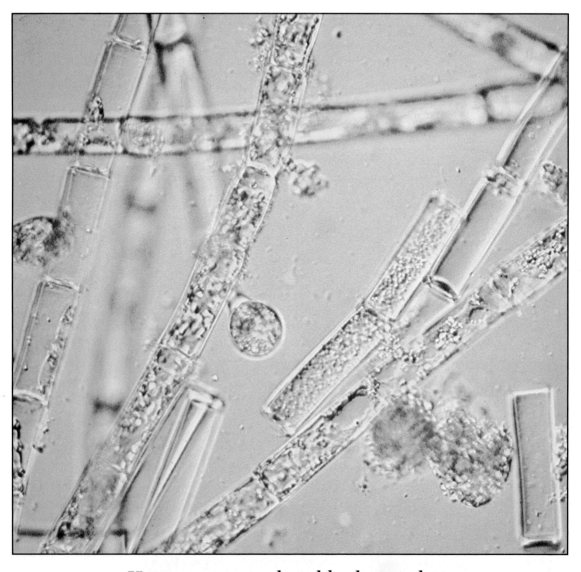

Here are some plant-like living things that live in a pond. They are very tiny. This picture was taken through a microscope. These plant-like living things are called **algae.** They do not have roots, stems, leaves, or flowers. They can make their own food. How are algae different from plants?

Some plants act like animals. This plant gets food in two ways. It is a green plant. It can make food in its leaves. But it can catch food, too. It is called a Venus' flytrap.

The leaves of a Venus' flytrap have tiny hairs. Insects touch the hairs. Then the leaves close tightly. The plant uses the insects for food.

ACTIVITY
Can fungi grow on food?

What to do

A. Rub some dust on a slice of bread.

B. Put the bread and a slice of apple in a plastic bag.

C. Put 10 drops of water in the bag. Close the bag.

D. Put the bag in a warm place. Look at it every day for 3 days.

What do you see?

1. What changes do you see on the food?

What do you think?

2. Tell if you think it is alive.

3. How do you know?

Most farmers work in the sun. These farmers do not. They work in a dark cave. The lights on their hats help them to see.

Mushrooms do not need sunlight. They grow best in dark, damp places. The farmers plant the mushrooms in trays. They add decaying plant and animal material to the trays. The mushrooms use these materials for food.

A Water Wonder—Grows Without Soil

In some places, the soil is too poor to grow crops. Scientists have found a new way to grow crops without using soil. This is helping people to eat better in places where the soil is poor.

Scientists have found a new way to grow plants using only water. They add things to plain water so that it has almost everything the plants need. It has food. It has air.

The Greek word for water is *hydro*. This new way of growing plants in water is called hydroponics.

Growing plants in water can be a good way to grow food. Plants can be grown outdoors or indoors. These plants usually produce more food than plants grown in soil.

What Do You Think?

Would growing plants in water be a good way to grow plants in space? Why or why not?

Chapter Review

Main Ideas

- Plants are living things.

- Plants need air, sunlight, soil, and water.

- Plants grow in many places.

- There are many kinds of plants.

Science Words

Use these words to fill in the blanks.

living things   **soil**   **fungi**
moss   **algae**

1. The roots of plants hold on to _____ .

2. _____, _____, _____ are living things.

3. All plants are _____ _____ .

Questions

1. Which objects are plants?

2. Can a green plant live in a cave?
   How do you know?

3. The park changed. How did it
   happen?

Science Project

Plant a kitchen garden. Put some soil
in an egg carton. Plant some herb seeds
in the soil. Put your garden near a sunny
window. Keep the soil damp. Use your
plants for cooking.

You know that a greenhouse is a place where green plants grow. Did you know that *greenhouse* is made by joining the words *green* and *house?* The word *greenhouse* is a compound word. A compound word is made when two words are written together as one word.

Read each compound word below. On a piece of paper, write the two words that make up each of the compound words. Use these words in a sentence to tell what each compound word means.

The first one has been done for you.

side walk   The sidewalk is at the *side* of the road where people can *walk* safely.

sidewalk	**sunlight**	**flytrap**
hillside	**underwater**	**wildflower**

In Chapter 11, you learned about the different parts of plants.

Look at the plants on page 232.

1. Name the three plant parts shown in this picture.

2. Which plant parts are not shown?

3. Tell about the job done by each part.

In Chapter 12, you learned about what plants need.

Look at pages 256, 257, 265, and 266.

4. What do green plants need to live?

5. How are fungi different from green plants?

6. How are algae different from green plants?

Chapter 13

Health

1.

ENERGY FOR OUR BODIES

Whether you are awake or asleep, your body uses **energy.** Walking, running, talking, and sleeping all use energy.

When you study, eat, or watch TV, your body does not move very much. Your body uses only a little energy. When you run, swim, or jump, your body uses a lot of energy. Which people are using more energy?

The energy your body needs comes from food. Meat, bread, milk, fruit, and vegetables are foods that give you energy and help you grow. By eating many kinds of healthful foods, you can get the energy you need and grow strong.

After a busy day, your body is tired. A good night's **sleep** is important. Getting enough sleep helps your body get ready for another busy day.

2.

SAFETY AFTER SCHOOL

School is over for the day. These children have gone to a playground. Playgrounds, parks, and yards are safe places to play. It is not safe to play in the street or between parked cars. It is not safe to play near water or empty buildings. Where is it safe to play near your home? What **safety rules** do you follow when you play outside?

279

Safety is also important when you play inside. Never play on stairs. You can fall and hurt yourself. Never play with tools. Use tools only with an adult.

Things used in the garden or for cleaning can hurt you. Do not breathe or taste these things.

Have you ever taken **medicine?** It can help you when you are sick. Medicine can also harm you. Never take medicine by yourself. Take only those medicines given to you by your parents, a caring adult, or a doctor.

SAY NO

TO PLAYING WITH MATCHES

Singing around a campfire is lots of fun. The fire makes things cozy and warm. But fires can also be very dangerous. A fire can burn down a building. A fire can hurt animals and people, too.

Matches and lighters can cause a harmful fire. If someone wants to give you matches, say no. Playing with matches is never safe. Matches should be used only by adults.

3.

SAFETY ON THE ROAD

Before riding your bicycle, make sure it is working properly. Your bicycle needs brakes that work. It also needs reflectors and a light for night riding.

Follow these safety rules when riding your bike on the road:

1. Ride on the far right side of the road.

2. Obey all traffic signs.

3. Use correct hand signals.

4. Watch for cars and trucks.

You should do these things to stay safe when riding in a car:

1. Always use a **seat belt.** Buckle up before the car moves.

2. Be sure the car doors are closed and locked.

3. Stay seated. Leave the belt on until the car stops.

Follow these school bus safety rules:

1. Wait for the bus in a safe place.

2. Keep your arms and head inside the bus window.

3. Talk quietly and stay in your seat.

4. Cross 10 feet in front of the bus.

5. Never go under or cross behind the bus.

ACTIVITY

What to do

A. Draw two shapes on red paper. Cut out the shapes.

B. Put small dots of glue on one shape.

C. Sprinkle silver glitter on the glue.

D. Place both shapes on a piece of black paper.

E. Turn off the lights. Shine a flashlight on the shapes.

What do you see?

1. Which shape is easier to see?

What do you think?

2. Which shape is like a bicycle reflector?

3. How can reflectors help keep you safe at night?

PEOPLE AND SCIENCE

Rain or shine, the school crossing guard stands at this busy street. The guard helps children cross safely.

Wait on the curb when you come to a street with a crossing guard. The guard will stop the cars. When it is safe, the guard will tell you to cross. Look both ways and then cross quickly.

Chapter Review

MAIN IDEAS

- Our bodies use energy every day.

- We should follow safety rules for play.

- We should follow safety rules on the road.

SCIENCE WORDS

The Science Words letters are mixed up. Write the words the right way.

1. We use a lot of *yerneg* when we run.

2. Our bodies need rest and *plees*.

3. Follow *efsaty lurse* when riding a bicycle.

4. Never take *eidmicen* by yourself.

QUESTIONS

1. Which person is using more energy?

2. How can you get the energy you need?

3. Where are two safe places to play?

4. Name two people you may take medicine from.

5. Name the school bus safety rules.

SCIENCE PROJECT

Find pictures of people staying healthy. Which pictures show people using a lot of energy? Which pictures show people getting enough sleep? Which pictures show people following safety rules?

SCIENCE WORD LIST

The science words are in alphabetical order. The number tells you on which page to find the word.

salty	195	size	151
scales	12	sleep	278
season	58	slower	152
seat belt	283	smooth	169
seeds	245	snow	52
shadow	129	soft	100
shallow	199	sound	95
shape	151	speed	152

PHOTO CREDITS

The following abbreviations indicate the position of the photograph on the page: *t,* top; *b,* bottom; *l,* left; *r,* right; *c,* center.

Russell Dian, Courtesy of the N.Y.C. Fire Department; 178, UPI Bettmann Newsphoto; 182, Victoria Beller-Smith.

Unit 5: 184,186, David Falconer, Bruce Coleman, Inc.; 185,208, Carl Roessler, Tom Stack & Associates; 187, Yoav Levy, Phototake; 188, Obromski, The Image Bank; 189, Grant Heilman; 190, Richard Haynes; 191*t*, Manuel Rodriguez; 191*b*, Breck P. Kent, Animals Animals; 192*t*, Peter Vadnai, Editorial Photo Color; 192*b*, Dan McCoy, Rainbow; 193, Ken Lax; 194, Russell Dian; 195, Guido Alberto Rossi, The Image Bank; 196*t*, Luis Villota, The Image Bank; 196*c,b*, Porter, Taurus Photos; 198, Russell Dian; 199, Arthur d'Arazien, The Image Bank; 200*t*, Russell Dian; 200*b*, Stephen Bower, Ocean Photographic Services, Inc., The Stock Market; 201, Alan Gurney, The Stock Market; 202, Yoav Levy, Phototake; 203, Richard Nowitz, The Image Bank; 204, Gene Ahrens, Bruce Coleman, Inc.; 209, R.F. Head, Animals Animals; 209 *inset*, R. Rowan, Photo Researchers, Inc.; 210, Grant Heilman; 211*t*, Ken Lax; 211*b*, Manfred Kage, Peter Arnold, Inc.; 212, John Lei, OPC; 213*tl*, John Lidington, Photo Researchers, Inc.; 213*tr*, Stephen Bower, The Stock Market; 213*bl*, G. Williamson, Bruce Coleman, Inc.; 213*br*, Chris Newbert, Bruce Coleman, Inc.; 214*t*, National Audubon Society, Photo Researchers, Inc.; 214*b*, Pat Morris, Ardea Photographers; 215*t*, Grant Heilman; 215*b*, Ardea Photographers; 216, John Lei, OPC; 217, Carl Roessler, Animals Animals; 220, Richard Haynes; 221, N.Y. Zoological Society; 222,223, Steve McCutcheon, Alaska Pictorial Service.

Unit 6: 228,230, Victoria Beller-Smith; 229,254, Steve Solum, Bruce Coleman, Inc.; 231, W.H. Hodge, Peter Arnold, Inc.; 233, Ken Lax; 234, Russell Dian; 235, Dan Guravich, Photo Researchers, Inc.; 236*t*, Webb Photos; 237, Ken Lax; 238,239, Russell Dian; 240, Christina Wohler; 241, A.J. Deane, Bruce Coleman, Inc.; 242, Ken Lax; 243, Russell Dian; 244*l*, Arthur d'Arazien, The Image Bank; 244*tr*, L. West, Photo Researchers, Inc.; 244*br*, John Bova, Photo Researchers, Inc.; 245,246, Ken Lax; 247*t*, Webb Photos; 247*b*, W.H. Hodge, Peter Arnold, Inc.; 248, Russell Dian; 249, Burpee; 249 *inset*, Louis Fernandez; 250*l*,251*c,r*, Runk/Shoenberger, Grant Heilman; 250*c,r*,251*l*, Grant Heilman; 255,256*b*, Ken Lax; 256*t*, Jay Lurie; 256*c*, Rona W. Tucullo; 257,258, Russell Dian; 259*l*, David Overcash, Bruce Coleman, Inc.; 259*r*, Robert L. Dunne, Bruce Coleman, Inc.; 260, Bill Swann; 261,262, Ken Lax; 263, Russell Dian; 264, H. Lloyd, The Image Bank; 265*tl*, Gil Fahey, Bruce Coleman, Inc.; 265*tr*, Michael P. Gadomski, Photo Researchers, Inc.; 265*bl*, Robert Lee, Photo Researchers, Inc.; 265*br*, Charlie Ott, Photo Researchers, Inc.; 266, E.R. Degginger, Animals Animals; 267*t*, A. Blank, Bruce Coleman, Inc.; 267*bl,br*, Breck P. Kent; 268, Russell Dian; 269, Butler County Mushroom Farm, PA; 270, Nancy Durrell McKenna, Photo Researchers, Inc.; 271, Grant Heilman; 274, William E. Ferguson; 276, Pat Field, Bruce Coleman, Inc.; 277, Jonathan Wright, Bruce Coleman, Inc.; 278, Victoria Beller-Smith; 279, Cecile Brunswick, Peter Arnold, Inc.; 280*t*, Ken Karp, OPC; 280*b*, Victoria Beller-Smith; 281*t*, Robert Semeniuk, The Stock Market; 281*b*, Group III, Bruce Coleman, Inc.; 282, 283*t*, Rick Browne; 283*b*, Ken Lax; 284, Victoria Beller-Smith; 285, Barbara Kirk, The Stock Market.

ART CREDITS

Robert Frank—pp. 41, 65, 146, 179, 205

Robert Filipowich, pp. 226

Jan Pyk—pp. 18, 19, 28–29, 33, 42, 43, 66, 67, 72, 88, 89, 107, 114, 115, 136, 137, 162, 163, 180, 181, 206, 207, 218–219, 224, 225, 252, 253, 272, 273

Joel Snyder—pp. 37, 38

Lane Yerkes—pp. 286, 287